The

Budget Book

Variety's On Production Series

Series Editor: Jerrold T. Brandt, Jr. Publisher,
Variety's On Production

The On Production Budget Book
Robert J. Koster

The ON PRODUCTION Budget Book

Robert J. Koster

Focal Press
Boston   Oxford   Johannesburg   Melbourne   New Delhi   Singapore

Focal Press is an imprint of Butterworth–Heinemann.

 A member of the Reed Elsevier group

 Butterworth–Heinemann supports the efforts of American Forests and the Global ReLeaf program in its campaign for the betterment of trees, forests, and our environment.

Library of Congress Cataloging-in-Publication Data

Koster, Robert.
 The on production budget book / by Robert J. Koster
  p.   cm.
 Includes index.
 ISBN 0–240–80298–5 (alk. paper)
  1. Motion pictures—Production and direction. 2. Motion picture industry—Finance. 3. Movie magic budgeting. I. Title.
 PN1995.9.P7K616 1997
 791.43′0232—dc21   97–19981
                                                    CIP

British Library Cataloguing-in-Publication Data
A catalogue record for this book is available from the British Library.

The publisher offers special discounts on bulk orders of this book.
For information, please contact:
Manager of Special Sales
Butterworth–Heinemann
313 Washington Street
Newton, MA 02158–1626
Tel: 617-928-2500
Fax: 617-928-2620

For information on all Focal Press publications available, contact our World Wide Web home page at: http://www.bh.com/focalpress

10 9 8 7 6 5 4 3 2 1

Printed in the United States of America

CONTENTS

Related Focal Press Titles

Filmmakers and Financing
Business Plans for Independents

Louise Levison

1994   232pp   Paperback   0-240-80207-1 $22.95

The Complete Film Production Handbook
Eve Light Honthaner

1996   400pp   Paperback (w/2 PC disks)   0-240-80236-5 $49.95

Pre-Production Planning for Video, Film, and Multimedia
Steve R. Cartwright

1996   240pp   Paperback (with disk)   0-240-80271-3 $34.95

Film Production Management
Bastian Clevè

1994   232pp   Paperback   0-240-80106-7 $28.95

Production Management for Film and Video, Second Edition
Richard Gates

1995   192pp   Paperback   0-240-51415-7 $32.95

Detailed information on these titles may be found in the Focal Press Catalog (Item #560). To request a copy, call 1-800-366-2665. You can also visit our web site at: http://www.bh.com/focalpress.

These books are available from all better book stores or in case of difficulty call: 1-800-366-2665 in the U.S. or +44 1865 310366 in Europe.

E-Mail Mailing List
An e-mail mailing list giving information on latest releases, special promotions/offers and other news relating to Focal Press titles is available. To subscribe, send an e-mail message to majordomo@world.std.com. Include in message body (not in subject line) subscribe focal-press.

INTRODUCTION

The process of budgeting has changed radically in the past few years. In the early 1960s when I first became a Production Manager it would take several days with a hand-cranked adding machine, pencils, and a lot of erasers, to create a decent budget.

Today since the advent of the better computer budgeting programs it takes only a few hours and some knowledge of copy-and-paste to enable the adept Production Manager to put together a budget. That and a thorough knowledge of the budgeting process.

This book is about the process of budgeting, specifically budgeting using a computer. There are several budgeting software programs in the marketplace which will make budgets for you, but of those only one has the lion's share of the market (well over 90%), and for good reason. Movie Magic is the only program that works on both IBM and Macintosh platforms, and the data are interchangeable between the two. No other program can make that statement as of this writing, or in the foreseeable future. Furthermore, Movie Magic seems to be designed most closely to the way we are accustomed to making budgets, and undoubtedly the designers and programmers listened to the plentiful advice given them by members of the film-making community.

While this book assumes that we are using a computer to budget the project, it is still written to enable the reader to learn all the principles of budgeting and the elements that must be taken into account, so the budget can still be made by hand if desired.

This is a combination book, part budgeting textbook and part user's manual. We will show how budgets are structured and the thought which goes into the building of each account; we also will show how to use Movie Magic Budgeting, enabling us to use our knowledge of budgeting as efficiently as possible.

Some folks need to be acknowledged here: Jerry Brandt, Publisher of *On Production Magazine*; Marie Lee, Tammy Harvey, Jodie McCune, without whose editing expertise this book would look awful and probably be unreadable; that paragon of syntactical excellence, Gnomi Gouldin, who deflated my happy bubble of belief in my own grammatical infallibility; the fine folks at Screenplay Systems who devised Movie Magic, especially Stephen Greenfield, whose work has brought so much efficiency to the movie industry scheduling and budgeting process; and my remarkably patient wife, Sarah, an absolute wizard at keeping food warm no matter how many times I tell her, "I'll be there in a minute, Dear."

BEFORE WE BEGIN

We need to make some assumptions.

1. We already own Movie Magic Budgeting. It is loaded onto our computer, or we will own it shortly.
2. If we're not using a computer, we have a budget blank, at least a chart-of-accounts, similar to the one presented in this book. That, in hard copy, and a plentiful supply of pencils and especially erasers.
3. We have a script and have analyzed each scene for those items that will cost money. In other words, we have made breakdown sheets. Movie Magic Scheduling is the best program to use for this process, partly because of its own facility, and partly because *Movie Magic Scheduling can import its information directly into Movie Magic Budgeting,* a process that will save us much time and effort.
4. We already have scheduled our project. There is no point in starting a budget without having scheduled the project. A budget is merely a reflection of how money will be spent over a period of time; the schedule tells us what that period of time will be. Obviously if an Actor is hired for two weeks we will be paying more than if we hire the same Actor for one day. The schedule tells us what those time elements are.

Now let's start budgeting.

BASIC PRINCIPLES

Budgeting elements seem to divide themselves into groups of three. I don't know why, but it happens.

1. The three main documents necessary for film production, the three main blueprints, if you will, are

    A. Script

    B. Schedule

    C. Budget

    Each of these is dependent on the others. When one changes it changes the rest. If the budget requirements change, we will have to adjust the script or schedule to accommodate that change. When the script changes, it necessarily changes the schedule and the budget.

2. The three levels of budget construction are

    A. Top sheet

    B. Category level

C. Account or detail level

The *Top Sheet* is the summary of all the levels of the budget that follow it. It lists all the categories, or major areas, of the budget, such as script, camera, and extras. The *Category* level opens the budget up to more minute work; each category contains several *Accounts,* which contain the lines of detail that make up the meat of the budget. At this level, the *Account* level, we enter the information that will add up to the summary on the top sheet. It is the only area into which figures can be entered.

3. The three main areas of the budget form are

A. Above the line

B. Production

C. Post-production

These are reflected on the *Top Sheet*, or the main summary document, of our budget. A fourth area, "Other," covers all those elements which don't fit naturally into the big three above.

4. The three main elements to budget for each account are:

A. Personnel

B. Tools

C. Material

For instance, the Wardrobe Department needs personnel, such as a Wardrobe Supervisor for men and one for women. Tools include the sewing machines, needles and thread, washing machines and the like. Materials such as fabric make up the costumes themselves, on which we use the tools to alter them for use in the picture. Tools generally belong to the crew members in each department, whereas materials generally are rented or purchased individually for each film and returned or sold after production is finished.

5. The three main phases of production are

A. Pre-production or "Prep"

B. Shoot

C. Wrap

These three phases must be considered in our budget. If we don't give our crew enough time to prepare the show, something will be missing on the first day of filming. For instance, consider the Wardrobe Department once again. The wardrobe people need plenty of time prior to filming to fit the costumes to the cast. So as soon as an Actor is cast in a role, that Actor must come to the office for fittings, long before the first day of filming, so the Director and Producer can see what the Actor looks like in the costumes and make adjustments if necessary. Nothing can be worse than making the entire shooting crew stand around while the wardrobe is adjusted because the wardrobe department was not given sufficient time to prepare the costume. By the same token, when the show is over we need to give the wardrobe crew time to return the clothes to the rental house. Having a member of our own Wardrobe Department present when the clothes are checked in is insurance against claims that pieces of wardrobe are missing and the resultant bills. This kind of thinking must be applied to each department and the budget must reflect the proper amount of prep and wrap time as necessary.

Also, please remember that when we make this first budget estimate it is far better to err on the plus side, not the minus side. A good rule of thumb is that no matter at what figure we budget our picture, the investors will almost inevitably tell us it's too much. Therefore, if we budget too little, we will be forced to remove some necessary items in order to get the money to produce the project. Better to be a little "fat."

Another big factor in the book is this: the template for the budget format is one I have designed for the Movie Magic budgeting system. I have simplified the budget form in several ways for readability. The rates in the budget are the union rates applicable at the time of writing. The budget form for the program contains non-union rates as well, but they would not be useful in this setting because of their immense variations between one company and the next.

I also have removed all the duplications that were redundant in printed material. In the original form, for instance, each truck in the transportation department had its own driver with all the detail lines available. For this book I left one driver to act as a representative of all. This eliminated about 20 pages of budget form. Further, I included only the rates for in-town filming in Los Angeles, not distant location rates. When we use the program we will use the proper Superbudget template, which will be up to date, or else we will be using the Industry Labor Guide (ILG) add-on, in which we will find the current rates. The ILG also has rates for other parts of the country and Canada; it is our best guide to labor rules and rates for the movie industry.

PREPARING TO BUDGET

First we must open our budget. Open the program by double-clicking on the "Movie Magic Budgeting" icon. When the program is open, we will see a blank opening screen.

This is only the top runner. The rest of our screen is blank. Take the mouse, move the arrow to "File" in the top menu in the upper left-hand corner and click on it once. From the drop-down menu, click on "Open." Then we will have this screen:

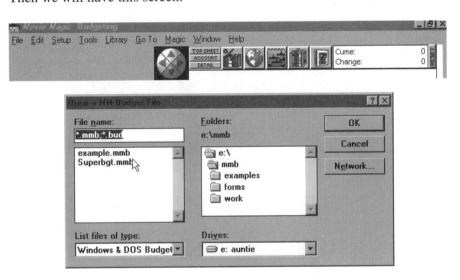

It is evident that I am about to click on the "Superbgt.mmb" in the dialogue box. Please double-click with the left mouse button. That will open up our budget for editing.

Now we will have a screen like this:

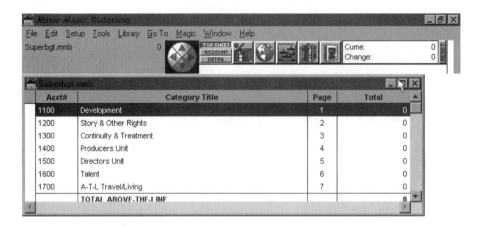

Obviously the area of information does not quite fill the screen. We have to *maximize* the screen so we can see what we're doing. So we put our mouse-arrow on the maximize button right here:

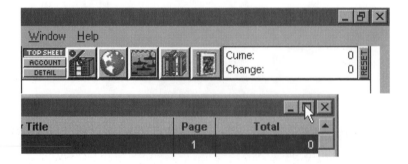

Click with the left mouse button once with the arrow on the maximize button, and the screen will fill with information like this:

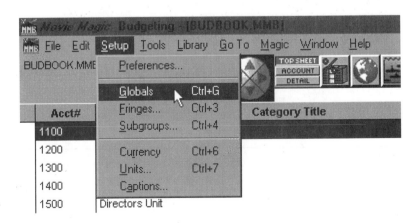

Acct#	Category Title	Page	Total
1100	Development	1	0
1200	Story & Other Rights	2	0
1300	Continuity & Treatment	3	0
1400	Producers Unit	4	0
1500	Directors Unit	5	0
1600	Talent	6	0
1700	A-T-L Travel/Living	6	0
	TOTAL ABOVE-THE-LINE		**0**
2100	Production Staff	8	0
2200	Art Direction	12	0
2300	Set Construction	14	0
2400	Set Decoration	17	0
2500	Property Department	19	0
2600	Camera Operations	21	0
2700	Electric Operations	24	0
2800	Grip Operations	25	0
2900	Production Sound	27	0
3000	Mechanical Effects	29	0
3100	Special Visual Effects	31	0
3200	Set Operations	31	0

We are now looking at the *top sheet* of the budget. The top sheet is the summary of all the information contained in the accounts at lower levels of the budget.

To prepare our budget for entering information we will make a giant leap into computer budgeting by telling our budget how long the shooting schedule is. We have already completed a shooting schedule using Movie Magic Scheduling, so we know how long our schedule will be. Let's say for the sake of this example that we will be shooting for four weeks on distant location, working six days a week, and for six weeks in town working five days a week.

We click on "Setup" in the main menu, then "Globals" in the drop-down menu.

That puts us into our "global" screen. Here we enter the shooting weeks: 4 in the "Equation" column opposite Shoot Local; 6 opposite Shoot Distant, and to keep our post-production figures straight we enter 20 opposite Post Prod.

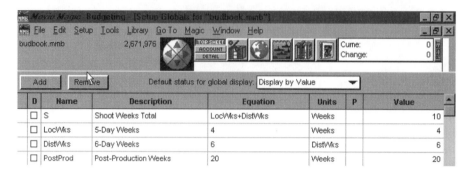

D	Name	Description	Equation	Units	P	Value
☐	S	Shoot Weeks Total	LocWks+DistWks	Weeks		10
☐	LocWks	5-Day Weeks	4	Weeks		4
☐	DistWks	6-Day Weeks	6	DistWks		6
☐	PostProd	Post-Production Weeks	20	Weeks		20

Now we further automate the budget by putting in the length of the completed film. For this we have to press the "End" key on the keyboard to drop to the bottom of the globals screen. Here we enter the film length. We have timed our script and found it to be 100 minutes long. Since 35mm film is projected at 90 feet/minute, 100 minutes works out to 9,000 feet. This works out to 9 reels. We enter that in the globals here:

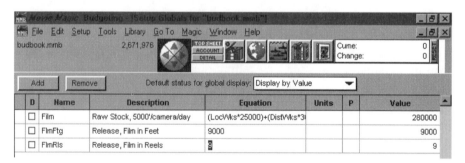

D	Name	Description	Equation	Units	P	Value
☐	Film	Raw Stock, 5000'/camera/day	(LocWks*25000)+(DistWks*3(			280000
☐	FlmFtg	Release, Film in Feet	9000			9000
☐	FlmRls	Release, Film in Reels	9			9

To have the budget calculate these figures we click on the lower of the two "X" boxes in the upper right corner of the screen:

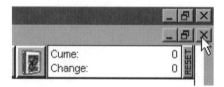

This begins the recalculation process which brings us back to the top sheet, but now we have the figures for our crew's shooting weeks and much more information entered automatically:

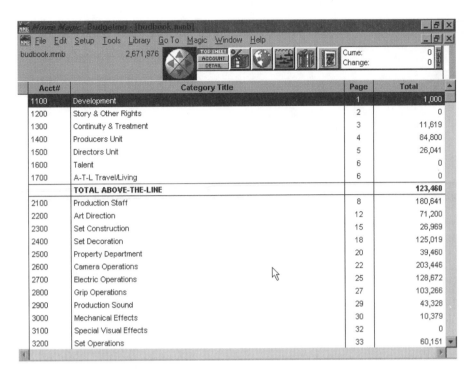

Next, we have to configure the rest of the budget to work within our shooting requirements. For this we must manipulate the "Subgroups" area. Let's assume that every member of the crew belongs to a Union. We have to go to the "Subgroups" and deselect the "Non-union" option. So we click on "Setup" in the upper menu, and on "Subgroups" in the dropdown menu:

This brings us to the "Subgroups" palette, where we have to deselect the "Non-Union" option:

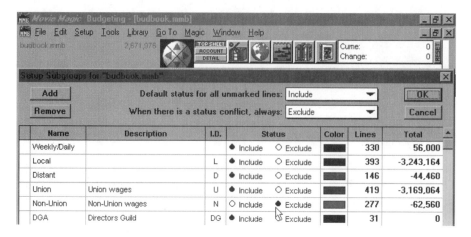

Good. Now we can click on the "OK" button in the upper right corner of the Subgroups palette to put our non-union exclusion into effect. What we have done is to dim out all the non-union areas of the Superbudget, making them unusable on the computer screen, and ensuring that they will neither print nor be calculated in the final budget.

Now we have only one more item to handle before actually beginning to budget: We have to set up the header for the top sheet and the first page. Here we will enumerate the main people of the picture and tell something about the budget itself. Like which revision of the budget we are showing. So we first click on "File" and "Print":

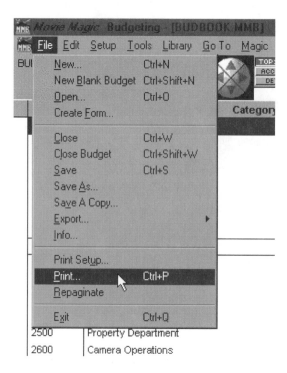

Now we have this screen:

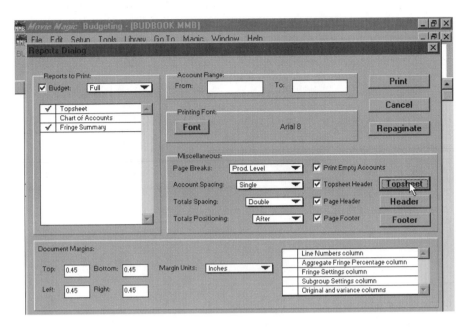

Note that we are about to click on "Topsheet." That will give us this:

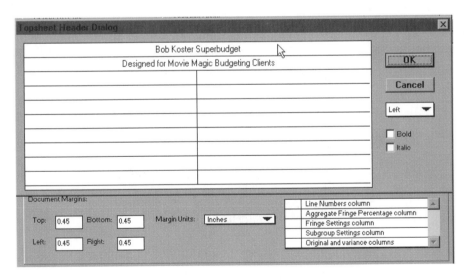

Here we enter the names of the Director and Producer, the revision number – all the information necessary to give the budget its logical informational framework so that anyone who reads it will know who is involved and on what basis it was made.

After we have filled in as many blanks as are appropriate we click on the little "OK" in the upper right corner, which brings us back to the top sheet.

Now that we have filled out the header, set the globals, and adjusted the subgroups, we can start budgeting in earnest.

To enter information in the budget we need to be on the *Account* or *Detail* level.

From here on we will be studying the elements in each account in detail. Just because an item is there does not mean that we have to use it, but it is always better to have these reminders of everything that might be necessary so we don't forget anything.

So from the top sheet, let's highlight our first account: Development.

1100 Development

> **Development** is what happens prior to funding. It can consist of story, options, research, even location scouting. But whatever it is, it usually is paid for by the Producer who will expect to be reimbursed when the project is given a "green light" by a studio or is funded by backers.

Let's enter the category by highlighting the line on the top sheet and clicking on the lower quadrant of our navigation globe.

This brings us to the *category* level, from which we can descend to the *account* level where we enter information.

Acct#	Account Title	Page	Total
1101	Story & Screenplay	1	1,000
1102	Producers Unit	1	0
1103	Directors Unit	1	0
1104	Budget Preparation	1	0
1105	Accounting	1	0
1106	Legal	1	0
1107	Office Overhead	1	0
1108	Transportation	2	0
1109	Research	2	0
1110	Travel/Living	2	0
1111	Additional Expenses	2	0
1198	Miscellaneous	2	0
1199	**Total Fringes**		**0**
	Total		**1,000**

We click once more on the lower quadrant of the navigation globe to get into the details:

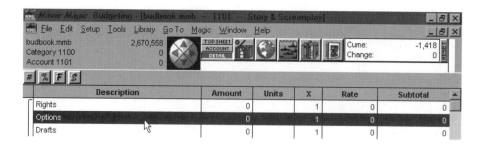

> **<u>Option</u>**: When we can't afford to buy the rights to a property but we know that we will be able to get the picture funded, we can buy an *option* to buy those rights within a certain period of time, say, six months or a year. The option will cost a small fraction of what the rights will cost. We are gambling that we will be able to get the project funded and in production before the option expires. The option agreement will give us the right to try to fund the project for *x* number of months. If, at the end of the option period, we have succeeded, we will then owe the writer the full price of the rights to the property. If we fail, we can buy an option extension for more money or let the property's rights revert to the writer who then can sell it to someone else. We will have lost the option money.

Now we click on "Options," because we have to enter the money we paid for the option on the script. We haven't bought the rights to it yet; just an option to buy the rights.

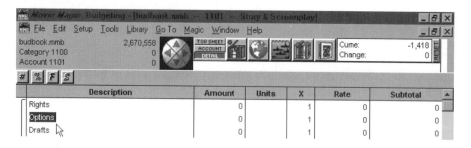

As we can see, we're ready to add figures. Press the "Tab" key to hop to the "Amount" field, and type "1." Tab again to the "Units" field, and press "A" for "Allow." We use the "Allow" unit whenever we are applying a figure over the entire length of the film, as opposed to "Weeks" or "Reels," etc. Now press "Tab" again, twice, to get to the "Rate" field. Here, let's assume that we are paying $1,000 for our option. Enter that figure. If we make a mistake we can always backtab by pressing "Shift + Tab" at the same time to tab backwards to the preceding fields. When we have entered the 1000 (we don't need to use the "$" or a comma), click outside of the chart area to stop the editing process. Our screen will now look like this:

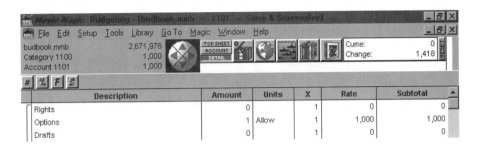

Good. We have increased the budget by $1,000 for the option. That is reflected in the control panel area at the top of the screen, where it says "Change," so we can track all our monetary changes to the budget as we go.

We may continue filling out the "Development" category in the same fashion, entering all the expenses we have incurred prior to funding.

Let's move on to the rest of the budget. First, let's go to the next account by clicking on "Top Sheet."

From the top sheet we can double-click on the next category, 1200, Story and Other Rights.

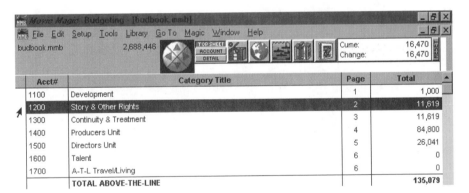

Which opens the category to us.

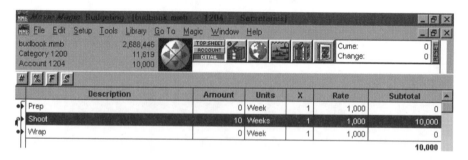

As we can see, we have already highlighted 1204, Secretaries Account. We have to rework this somewhat, because the Story Category in our script needs no secretary. We will reduce the figure here to 0. We click on the lower quadrant of our navigation globe to get into the secretary account.

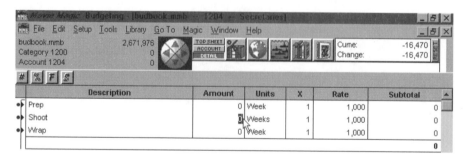

Now we highlight the "Shoot" detail line, press the "Tab" key to open the account for editing, and we tab over to the "Amount" field, where we substitute "0" for the entry. This will empty the account.

Now let's discuss the account.

1200 Story and Other Rights

Acct#	Account Title	Page	Total	
1201	Story Rights Purchase	2	0	
1202	Writers Fees	2	0	
1203	Story Consultant/Editor	2	0	
1204	Secretaries	2	0	
1205	Research	3	0	
1206	Typing	3	0	
1207	Duplication	3	0	
1298	Miscellaneous	3	0	
1299	**Total Fringes**		**0**	
	Total		**0**	

Every motion picture, no matter how primitive, must start with an idea. The idea might come from a book, a play, an original screenplay, a magazine article, a news story, or even a story told over dinner. At some point the Producer will have to pay someone for the rights to film the story. Even if it is our own story, there must still be provision in the budget for the production to legally reimburse the originator for the rights. Remember, the legal minimum payment is one dollar.

1201 Story Rights Purchase
This area covers the rights to the story, not the screenplay. It can be for the purchase of book rights, a short story from a magazine, or a payoff for our sister-in-law who just heard the cutest thing down at the hairstylist's.

1203 Story Consultant/Editor
This item is normally used during the "development" of a project. A writer might be an excellent novelist, perfectly capable of fashioning a marvelously readable book which became a best-seller, yet still fall short as a screen writer. Writing a piece to be read and writing a piece to be seen require two entirely different writing skills.

1205 Research
This area of research is for the original story, and covers such items as travel and living arrangements for writers when they have taken themselves to the deserts of Outer Mongolia in search of a good screenplay. This can also cover dinners for our Police Informant.

1206-07 Typing and Duplication
These items serve to reimburse the writer for his out-of-pocket expenses.

Fringe Benefits: There is an appendix at the end of this book which explains Fringe Benefits in detail.

1300 Continuity and Treatment

Acct#	Account Title	Page	Total
1301	Writers	3	0
1302	Research	3	0
1303	Typing	3	0
1304	Duplication	3	0
1305	Travel & Living	3	0
1306	Story Editor	3	0
1307	Consultants	3	0
1308	Legal Clearances	3	0
1309	Secretaries	3	10,000
1310	Office Expenses	3	0
1311	Entertainment	3	0
1312	Script Timing	3	0
1398	Miscellaneous	3	0
1399	**Total Fringes**		**1,619**
	Total		**11,619**

After we have purchased the rights to make a movie out of the original story, a workable screenplay must be fashioned. In theatrical ventures this will consist of scene descriptions and dialogue. If our project is a TV commercial the script often will consist of a storyboard.

Dialogue: Written manifestations of the spoken word.

1301 Writer
"Writers" in this account are the people who write the actual screenplay, not the original story (see Accounts 1200-02). Where that is the same person, two figures usually are negotiated, one for story and the other for screenplay.

1302 Research
If a screenplay needs more research than was done for the book, for instance, to provide further details for the art department, the screen writer must be paid (or reimbursed) for accomplishing this.

1305 Travel and Living Expenses
If we have paid for the screenwriter to stay in a bungalow at the Beverly Hills Hotel while our script is being written, this is where that expense goes. It also can cover research trips to observe the herding rituals of the nomads in Uzbekistan, when necessary.

1306 Story Editor
The "Story Editor" heads up the story department. In the case of episodic TV it refers to the very busy person who repairs all the weird

scripts that come in over the transom and makes them filmable. This could also be the person in charge of the group of stalwarts who do that.

1307 Consultants

When we write a screenplay and need information not available from the usual sources, such as libraries, we need the help of an expert in the field (or, at times, someone who passes himself off as an expert). This could be the subject of the biography we are writing, or the widow or widower of that subject, or a police officer involved in the hostage situation we are depicting. These people should be paid an honorarium which could be as little as $1.00 or as much as, well, you name it.

1308 Legal Clearances

When we have obtained written permission from the owner of a building or the owner's legally appointed agent to photograph the property, it is called "clearing" a location. Failure to do so can cost us a great deal of money in lawsuits.

Clearance: A means of ensuring that the use of names, pictures, locations, and so forth, is legal.

When the screenplay is complete, it will be necessary for us to check all the names of people and places to ensure that, if the story is fictitious, we have not unwittingly named our villain after the mayor of the town we thought was fictitious. Lawsuits have ensued because this simple procedure was not followed. A surprising number of people have in-laws who are attorneys and just itching to get their hands on the entire income of our movies for their clients. Also, please refer to the Errors and Omissions section of the Insurance Account of the budget for further comment on this (Account 6105).

1311 Entertainment

Our screenwriter may have to buy dinner and a small libation for a source of information to make him or her more informative. Well, we wanted the story to be realistic, didn't we?

1312 Script Timing

We may wish to have the script timed as soon as the screenwriter has come close to a working draft of the piece, just to make sure that we have no unpleasant surprises such as a 45-minute long feature film. This would normally be done at the beginning of pre-production, but there are a few odd cases in which the timing should be done far earlier. It's cheap insurance (also see Account 2113).

1400 Producers

Acct#	Account Title	Page	Total
1401	Executive Producer	4	0
1402	Producer	4	0
1403	Co-Producer	4	0
1404	Line Producer	4	0
1405	Supervising Producer	4	0
1406	Coordinating Producer	4	0
1407	Associate Producer	4	0
1408	Production Executive	4	0
1409	Secretaries	4	76,000
1410	Office Expenses	4	0
1411	Research	4	0
1412	Packaging Fee	4	0
1498	Miscellaneous	4	0
1499	**Total Fringes**		**8,800**
	Total		**84,800**

MMB Movie Magic Budgeting - [BUDBOOK.MMB - 1400 - Producers Unit]
File Edit Setup Tools Library Go To Magic Window Help
BUDBOOK.MMB 2,671,976 Category 1400 84,800 — TOP SHEET ACCOUNT DETAIL — Cume: 0 Change: 0

> The term **Producer** has many possible meanings. In the days when the Studio System ruled, the Producer was the ultimate financial authority on a film. At present, the word usually denotes a "gatherer." The producer puts together a script, Director, Actors, money – all in a package designed to appeal to the widest possible audience.

There are many different Producer credits – just look at any TV Movie of the Week and you'll see ten or more. Here are some of the more widely used:

1401 Executive Producer
In most cases the Executive Producer provides the money for production either from his or her own pocket or by collecting it from investors.

1402-03 Producer and Co-Producer
These credits in the TV world commonly refer to the heads of the Story Department of the series. On a TV series nothing can be worse than having no script ready in time for production. A crew standing around waiting for the script to be finished is not an inspiring sight. So the head writers are given better credits than on most productions as a small incentive to get the scripts finished in a timely fashion.

1404-05-06, Line Producer, Coordinating Producer, Supervising Producer
All these titles refer to the same basic function. Line Producer bridges the gap between the aesthetic and the financial. He or she works very closely with the Production Manager and Assistant Directors, as well as

with the writers and producers. Line Producers generally stay close to the shooting set to work with the Director and Production Team when decisions have to be made, for instance, to shorten scenes for schedule purposes. Line Producers can also be a great help in dealing with upper-echelon folks when necessary. I remember quite vividly an episodic TV show on which I was First Assistant Director. The Executive Producer was on the set with a laptop computer and insisted on rewriting scenes we had already filmed. The Line Producer gently led the man back to the office where he could interrupt the filming no longer.

1407 Associate Producer

An Associate Producer in the classic sense is in charge of post-production. I have also known cases in which the Associate Producer is the Screenwriter, or the Editor, whose contracts provided for Associate Producer credit. Sometimes this credit is given to what we would usually call the Line Producer.

1408 Production Executive

Two or three of the major studios and larger independent companies have Production Executives on their staffs. Production Executives act as liaisons between the production company, such as Disney, and the shooting company. Some companies assign one Production Executive to each project, and others assign one to several projects. The sole purpose of some Production Executives is to determine if productions are "producible" at all. Production Executives usually work closely with the Unit Production Manager, but report back to the studio daily on the progress of the film. Generally speaking the function is not covered by the Directors Guild of America (DGA), although a few Production Executives are members of the DGA.

1409 Secretaries

Description	Amount	Units	X	Rate	Subtotal
Prep	5	Weeks	4	1,000	20,000
Shoot	10	Weeks	4	1,000	40,000
Wrap	4	Weeks	4	1,000	16,000
					76,000

A Producer without a Secretary is like a day without sunshine. So if our project has four Producers of various kinds we have to account for their Secretaries in the budget. So let's highlight the Secretaries Account (1409) and drop down into it by mouse-clicking on the navigation ball.

Now we can add the right number of secretaries. First we press the "Tab" key to open the account for editing; then we insert in the "Amount" field some prep, let's say five weeks, and four weeks of wrap time. Then we go to the "x" field and change all the numbers to "4" to indicate that there are four secretaries:

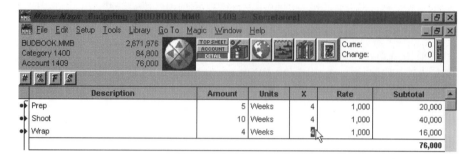

Notice that the figures are multiplied across the row horizontally. 4 × 4 × 1000 = 16,000. And the "Amount" field always refers to the number of "Units," in the next column; "x" in the column after that refers to the number of secretaries, grips, or affords another field for multiplication as we shall see in the post-production area.

1500 Director

Acct#	Account Title	Page	Total
1501	Director	5	0
1502	Directors Assistant	5	12,500
1503	Choreographer	5	0
1504	Dialogue Coach	5	0
1505	Secretary	5	10,000
1506	Storyboard Artist	5	0
1507	Office Expenses	5	0
1508	Travel/Living	5	0
1509	Second Unit Director	5	0
1598	Miscellaneous	5	0
1599	**Total Fringes**		**3,541**
	Total		**26,041**

The Director is the aesthetic sensibility behind the film. Everything on the screen is there because it has been filtered through the eyes and mind of the Director. What we see on the screen is the way the Director sees the story, from script through camera angles to editing.

1501 Director

A Director is the one person who bears the aesthetic responsibility of a film. No matter what the reviews say, the Director alone molds the film to fit his or her vision of the script. The Director works with the actors on their interpretations of the roles; works with the Cameraman on choice of lenses, angles and lighting moods; and most importantly, works with the Editor in choosing the assembly of shots, their order and their timing.

Except for Episodic TV shows and a few other types of show, the Director usually is paid a fee rather than a salary. Many Directors have loan-out corporations and are paid through those.

Loan-Out: A corporation through which a Director or major Star receives his or her income. The Producer contracts with the Loan-out company for the Director's services; the Loan-out company is the employer of record. If the employee makes sufficient money each year to warrant such an arrangement, it can be a big help. But many people do it whose incomes cannot support a loan-out, just because it is the current "in" arrangement, and the IRS frowns on such activity quite severely.

NOTE: Some Guilds are insisting on direct payment of fringe benefits by the Producer. This assures the Guilds that their records of members' incomes are correct. The Producer then reports to the Guild the employee's income, even if paid to a Loan out company, and Employer's share of Pension, Health and Welfare benefits are paid directly to the Guild or Union, not to the Loan-out company.

1502 Director's Assistant

This person is not the Assistant Director – that is another job altogether. This person is a personal assistant to the Director, keeps the Director's notes in order, reminds the Director of important appointments, and sometimes goes to the dry cleaners to pick up the Director's pants.

1503 Choreographer

This person, who designs the dance numbers and coaches the dancers in how to do them, is also part of the Director's team. Don't forget to give the Choreographer enough time to design the dance numbers and prepare for the filming. Rehearsals must also be scheduled. Prep is very important here. Wrap almost always is unnecessary.

1504 Dialogue Coach

Dialogue Coach refers to a person who helps with the dialogue. It can be the person who draws up the cue cards, or the person who rehearses lines with the actors. In the case of a foreign Actor with a thick accent, the studio may assign a dialogue coach to assist the Actor with the proper American inflection and pronunciation. It can also be a person who coaches an American Actor in foreign accents.

> **Dialogue**: The spoken word. Even if it is a monologue we call it dialogue.

> **Cue Card**: A plain white 4' 6' card on which the dialogue is printed in large letters and held in plain view of the forgetful Actor but out of camera range

On one show the Dialogue Coach was paid to make up cue cards for the Actor and rehearse him between shots, and that was all he did. The two worked very admirably as a team for many years, and the Actor insisted that that particular dialogue coach be written into his contracts.

1506 Storyboard Artist

At times a Director will need a story board artist to sketch out a particularly involved sequence because of action or effects or a combination. Sometimes the Art Director will personally make the story boards.

> **Storyboard**: A sort of comic-strip style depiction of an action sequence in which each frame depicts one shot.

1509 Second Unit Director

The Second Unit Director is more often than not the Stunt Coordinator. (see Account 1604) Sometimes a special Second Unit Director is called in to direct a particular sequence. Andrew Marton, for instance, directed the famous "Chariot Race" sequence in *Ben Hur*. The chariot race sequence was such a complicated logistical problem that it was almost like shooting a whole movie all by itself.

1598 Miscellaneous

Director's Buy-Out

When we "buy out" a Director, we are paying a large sum of money at once in the hope that he or she will never come back to us for any other payments such as residuals, etc. Sometimes this works.

1600 Cast

Acct#	Account Title	Page	Total
1601	Principal Roles	6	0
1602	Supporting Roles	6	0
1603	Day Players	6	0
1604	Stunt Gaffer	6	0
1605	Assistant Stunt Gaffer	6	0
1606	Stunt Players	6	0
1607	Stunt Doubles	6	0
1608	Utility Stunt Players	6	0
1609	Casting Expenses	6	0
1610	Screen Tests	6	0
1611	Overtime/Turnaround	6	0
1612	Musicians	6	0
1613	Looping	6	0
1614	Second Run Residuals (TV)	6	0
1615	Welfare Worker/Teacher	6	0
1616	Rehearsal Expenses	6	0
1617	Contractuals	6	0
1698	Miscellaneous	6	0
1699	**Total Fringes**		**0**
	Total		**0**

In theatrical ventures the most visible attribute of a show is its cast. Publicity surrounds their social lives, and a star with more exposure usually can command a higher salary than one with less exposure in the media. Naturally one would wish to hire an Actor with immense exposure and immense talent, availing oneself of the best of all possible worlds.

"Letters of Intent" from prospective cast members stating that they have read the script and are willing to consider employment on the project routinely are used to raise money for projects as yet unfunded. Even though the presence of a major star does not guarantee income for a movie, it certainly can't hurt. By the same token many movies have become great successes without major stars in the cast. It all comes down to that incredibly fickle entity, the public taste.

We must be sure when we hire an Actor that he or she is able to perform the actions in the script. More than once I have had to tie an Actor to a horse despite assurances that he or she could ride. I have hired dancers who had no rhythm, ice skaters who were often prone, and singers who were tone deaf.

1601 Stars
There is an enormous range of salaries given to stars, depending on such things as profit participation, time of filming and other perks, so it is impossible to assign a blanket allowance for remuneration in this case. The highest paid stars will demand and get $20 million dollars for appearing in a

single movie. Very low-budget pictures can pay Screen Actors Guild (SAG) scale plus a free lunch. Actors range anywhere in between, and some exceed even these limits.

In general, however, we consider that the Stars of the "Principal Cast" will be those few actors who have run-of-the-picture contracts. That is to say, they will be paid an agreed amount for acting in the picture whether it be for two days or three months, regardless of whether the Actor does not appear on set for long periods during the course of filming but is "on hold."

1602 Supporting Cast

Supporting Players are understood to be those actors who are working for four days or more (my own generalization), up to several weeks, but who do not have the status of Stars. Some of these might also have loan-out companies which we should treat as we have treated the Director's loan-out. Once the Director's loan-out has been set, our management of the other loan-outs should follow suit.

1603 Day Players

Day Players are Actors with scripted lines who work for three days or less. As a rule, when we are on distant location, we can usually cast most Day Players from local talent. Just have the casting people check around at the local little theatre groups and Theatre Arts Departments of local colleges and universities. You'll find plenty of good talent. Also try local TV stations.

1604 Stunt Gaffer

If our show has a number of stunts in it or even one very difficult stunt, it is wise to hire a Stunt Gaffer. A qualified Stunt Man with years of experience not only can save money but also lives or pain. This person will know whom to hire for particular stunts. Some Stunt Gaffers specialize in underwater work, fire, motorcycle stunts, and so on. It is not unusual for the Stunt Double for the Principal Actor to work as Stunt Gaffer as well. And if the main character is a lady, there are many highly qualified female Stunt Gaffers who will serve.

Gaffer: Someone who is in charge of a particular activity. We say that the person "gaffs" that activity. This practice began with the original lighting technicians, who used a hooklike device at the end of a long pole to manipulate the flags and scrims that shade the lights when they are very high off the ground. The device looked like the "Gaff" that fishermen use to bring in a big fish, so the name "Gaffer" was applied, and stuck. In current parlance it means "The Head of the Department." we can have a "Stunt Gaffer" and "Teamster Gaffer" too. The word "Gaffer" used alone traditionally means the head of the Electric Department.

A Note on Set Safety

There is never an excuse for any set injury or pain. It's only a movie. When stunts are happening, our trust should be placed in the stunt gaffer to prepare the stunt and execute it to the Director's specifications. Never change the Stunt Gaffer's plan without her or his knowledge. And while the stunt is in progress the Stunt Gaffer will run the set. Do not ever try to do this yourself. Injuries happen that way. Set Safety is discussed more thoroughly in Account 2123.

1606 Stunt Players

Stunt Players are those faceless stunt persons who make the stunts more interesting. Ever see a scene where someone is careening down the road, out of control, and the other cars are swerving to avoid the maniac? Well, the drivers of those other cars all are stunt people too, specially trained in car stunts. As responsible producers we certainly cannot trust those cars to the hands of anyone else.

1607 Stunt Doubles

These folks are about the same size, shape and coloring as the Actors they replace for the difficult scenes. Don't forget that, when an Actor has to be "doubled" for a scene, the Stunt Double needs to be fitted for wardrobe as well. We don't want the crew standing around waiting while an Actor disrobes and a stunt double changes into his clothes. Also, be wary of actors who want to do their own stunts, which is most of them. Stunt doubles are better. Actors usually are not good at stunts and could get hurt. If that happens production ceases until the cast is removed and the Actor can work again. That's what stunt doubles are for.

1608 Utility Stunt Players

Stunt people trust nobody more than other stunt people, especially those with whom they have worked before. I once filmed a stunt in which an Actor, who was on fire, had to leap three stories into a safety air-bag inside a shopping mall. We had three stunt people at the third floor level holding fire extinguishers and four more on the ground floor with extinguishers and paramedics. These people never appeared on camera; they just acted as safety backup for the stunt. They were paid a normal day rate.

Stunt Adjustments: Those sums of money given to stunt persons for performing hazardous or difficult stunts. The amount varies according to the difficulty of the stunt, and the rate is always negotiated prior to filming the shot. Stunt people earn SAG minimum plus their stunt adjustments.

1609 Casting Office

Description	Amount	Units	X	Rate	Subtotal
Videotape System	1		1	0	0
Postage, Messengers	1		1	0	0
Computer charges	1		1	0	0
Office assistants	1		1	0	0
Total					**0**

The people who cast a film are important to maintaining its quality. At times, it is worth the few extra dollars we pay a first-class casting person to get a top-flight cast. The money we save in cast salaries and contracts will more than cover the higher rates.

Videotape System
We will want to have a videotape system in our office. At its simplest, this can consist of a VHS playback dummy and a monitor. Most agents keep videotapes of their clients' latest shows on "sample reels," which they will send to our office for viewing. Many agents who handle Cameramen and Art Directors also have sample reels of their work. Viewing the prospective cast's work like this will save a great deal of time in interviews.

Also the Producer or Director may wish to go to New York to cast from Broadway. At such times it may be cost effective to have a New York Casting person videotape prospective actors and send the tapes us for viewing before personal interviews are set up in New York.

Computer
Many times the casting people will use a computer to store information about performers. Naturally we will be expected to pay for the computer and its supplies.

1610 Screen Tests
Because of the extensive use of videocassettes in the casting process very few screen tests are filmed any more. However, just in case we want one, the account is here.

1611 Overtime and Turnaround
Turnaround is the time between the end of work on one day and beginning of work the next. In the case of actors Turnaround is usually twelve hours with a few exceptions. This means that an Actor who wraps at 10:00 PM one evening cannot be called back to work until after 10:00 AM the next morning, or we will have to pay a very heavy penalty for "Forcing" the call by "invading" the turnaround hours. This is where we put our best estimate for such overtime costs.

> <u>**Wrap**</u>: The end of filming for a day.

1612 Musicians

"Musicians," in this context, are those folk who stand at the side of the set and make music while the actors emote. Usually, they play music to accompany the actors on camera who are miming playing music with instruments that are mute. A far easier system is to use "Playback," covered in the sound department, under Account 2905.

> <u>**Cartage**</u>: The transport of the instruments from the instrument rental place to the studio and back.

1613 Looping

This refers to Automatic Dialogue Replacement, which we treat at length in the Post-Production Sound Account 5303.

1615 Welfare Worker/Teacher

> The law in most states of the United States requires that when we hire minors we must follow very strict guidelines. This is *law*, not tradition, and the penalties for not observing the law are very severe indeed:
>
> 1. Your company *must* have a permit to employ minors.
> 2. The minor *must* have a permit to work from the state.
> 3. The minor may work only within certain hours and only for certain numbers of hours depending on age and school requirements. These hours are explained elsewhere, notably in the Industry Labor Guide.
> 4. Each minor *must* have a guardian or family member present at all times during work hours.
> 5. A Welfare Worker licensed by the state *must* be present for schooling and to watch after the student's schooling.
>
> The state keeps lists of licensed welfare workers who will help us. But the important thing is that the worker *must* be present before we can have a minor on set.

1615 Contractuals

Actors have the funniest contracts. Many contain stipulations that nobody in the real world would ever request, "perks" that under normal circumstances would be considered outrageous. In our business, however, they are merely eccentric. These are the famous Contractuals, and since they will have to be paid for somehow, they have to be a part of our budget.

For example, on one TV series, one Actor had written into the contract that he would not have to work past noon on Friday, he would be driven to the airport where a studio-supplied airplane waited to fly him to his ranch in Arizona. On Sunday evening the plane would fly him back to Hollywood.

All this had to be accounted for in the budget. Another Actor contractually had to be provided with a specific year of a specific estate-bottled wine, along with the specific style of Lalique crystal glasses from which to drink it. Maybe it was Orrefors crystal – it was a long time ago.

One very famous Actor recently was paid $15 million for one movie, and the "contractuals" amounted to another $3 million. The Actor would not do the movie without them.

1700 Above-the-Line Travel and Living

Acct#	Account Title	Page	Total
1701	Hotels	6	0
1702	Travel	6	0
1703	Per Diem	7	0
1704	Car Rentals	7	0
1705	Misc. Expenses	7	0
1799	**Total Fringes**		**0**
	Total		**0**

Most of the time when I am doing a budget I put all the travel and living figures into the Location Account 3500. But different producers have different habits regarding where various items are to be budgeted, so an account for Travel and Living for the above-the-line folks is here for your convenience.

Above-the-Line Notes

This completes the above-the-line section of the budget. The industry-accepted definition of *above-* and *below-the-line* traditionally places all the artistic sections above the line and the mechanical or "crafts" sections below it. That is a very broad generalization, born in the early days of film-making when a Cameraman was hired because he could crank consistently and an Editor was known as a "Cutter." If it were still strictly true, our Cameraman and Editor would be above the line and their assistants would be below the line. I have seen budget forms in which there was provision for Music both above- and below-the-line. I have seen Cast put below the line, and Extras above it. I have seen entire production departments above the line, DGA trainees included. No budget form is universally accepted, but this one does follow generally accepted industry practice.

2100 Production Staff

Acct#	Account Title	Page	Total
2101	Production Manager	8	52,046
2102	Unit Production Manager	8	14,164
2103	First Assistant Director	8	13,108
2104	2nd Assistant Director	8	8,980
2105	2nd 2nd Assistant	9	0
2106	Other Assistants	9	0
2107	DGA Trainees	9	2,156
2108	Production Associates	9	1,600
2109	Technical Advisor	9	0
2110	Production Coordinator	9	4,483
2111	Ass't Prod. Coord.	9	2,608
2112	Local Prod. Coord.	10	0
2113	Script Supervisor	10	5,667
2114	Production Auditor	10	7,713
2115	Ass't Production Auditor	10	4,277
2116	Payroll Secretary	11	0
2117	Local Auditor	11	0
2118	Location Manager	11	7,676
2119	Ass't Location Mgr	11	2,964
2120	Interpreters	11	0

For proper logistics, scheduling, and general budget supervision the Production Department is our most valuable tool. Great care must be taken in the selection of personnel here, because these folks will make hiring decisions in all other departments.

2101   Production Manager

Description	Amount	Units	X	Rate	Subtotal
DGA:	1		1	0	0
Prep	0	Week	1	4,000	0
Shoot	4	Weeks	1	4,000	16,000
Wrap	0	Week	1	4,000	0
Prep Distant	0	Weeks	1	5,000	0
Shoot Distant	6	Weeks	1	5,000	30,000
Wrap Distant	0	Weeks	1	5,000	0
Production Fee - Local	4	Weeks	1	541	2,164
Production Fee - Distant	6	Weeks	1	647	3,882
Severance	0	Flat	1	4,000	0
					52,046
Computer Rental	0	Week	1	0	0
Computer Supplies	0	Week	1	0	0
Car Allowance	0	Week	1	0	0
Total					**52,046**

MMB Movie Magic Budgeting - [BUDBOOK MMB - 2101 - Production Manager]
File Edit Setup Tools Library Go To Magic Window Help
BUDBOOK MMB   2,671,976   TOP SHEET / ACCOUNT / DETAIL   Cume: 0
Category 2100   160,641   Change: 0
Account 2101   52,046

A Production Manager does just that – he or she manages the production. As a Production Manager, I have begun working with a Producer when all he or she had was a script and a promise from a studio to back his production. I have broken the script down, scheduled it, worked out a budget, submitted the budget to the studio, and reworked it until the studio felt comfortable with it. Then I have rented office space, hired secretaries, rented office furniture and equipment such as computers, Xerox and fax machines, and the like. I have hired the crew, arranged for Union contracts, supervised the clearances of locations, casting, all the time keeping the budget up to date as to the estimates and current status. I have supervised the filming, worked with the Director to keep the budget under control, kept the logistics running smoothly with the film (or tape) labs, and so forth.

After filming was finished I released the crew, kept track of the editing process, music recording, Foley, and so on, all the while paring down the office space and equipment rental to exactly what was necessary and no more. In general a Production Manager should be capable of running a production from the time the script is finished until the delivery of the final cut to the studio or network.

In short, the Production Manager (PM) runs the day-to-day business of the company. Makes the budget, then helps everyone to live within its limits.

The rates shown here are rough averages for almost every department. There will be times when we will pay far more than I have shown here and times when we will pay far less. I recently saw a budget for a very low-budget picture (non-DGA) in which the Production Manager was budgeted at $1250.00 a week. When it gets that low our best bet is to go to the

Theater Arts department of a local college and hire someone who has never done it before, then pray a great deal.

Another thing to bear in mind is that when filming is local and the crew is living at home and working five days a week, the rates are less than on location in East Horses Breath, Montana, and working six days a week.

It is in the interest of the company to give all the members of the crew as much preparation time as necessary. Prep time is when we save money – the better prepared we are, the easier the shoot will be. Rule of thumb for the PM or Unit Production Manager (UPM): at least 1 1/2 times the shoot period for prep. For a 10-week shoot, better give the PM 15 weeks prep to get the show prepared properly. The PM also needs wrap time. After the shoot is over someone has to make sure the bills are correct and paid; keeping the PM on for wrap is cheap insurance against some rental house rip off.

PM – Production Fee
A Production Fee is a DGA contractual payment for the Production Manager and First and Second Assistant Director DGA members who work while the camera is rolling. It is not uncommon for the larger companies to pay the production fee whether filming is occurring or not, as a slight over scale compensation.

PM – Severance
Severance, also called "Completion of Assignment Fee," also is a DGA contractual payment, amounting to one week's pay, covering the time our DGA employees need to find a job when production is over.

Computer Rental
Here we obviously have a choice. Normally our PM will bring in his or her own computer and charge us rental for it. It is money well spent. We also may rent a computer for the PM from a computer rental house.

2102 Unit Production Manager (UPM)
The terms Production Manager and Unit Production Manager have become almost interchangeable over the years, but there is a difference. A Production Manager manages all the productions for a given company. In major studios, the title may be Executive Vice President in Charge of World-Wide Production or some such thing, but the function is to manage the total production for that company. Under the PM there may be several "units" or individual shooting companies, each working on a single project. Each single project has its own Unit Manager or Unit Production Manager, responsible for that project alone.

Starting with the Unit Manager, I have assumed that we will be paying DGA Guild minimum wages. I also have assumed that these people all will be on the regular payroll and that none has a loan-out company. If they do have loan-out companies, we may have to rework the figures slightly to reflect that fact.

2103   First Assistant Director

A First Assistant Director (A.D.) is the Sergeant Major, the efficiency expert who makes sure that the set is functioning smoothly. He or she starts doing that by designing a shooting schedule that maximizes the time use value of the crew, cast, and Director. After that, running the set efficiently and being flexible when problems arise are of paramount importance – that and set safety. A section on safety is part of Account 2123.

The First A.D. always stays on the set next to the camera while production is in process. This person is the communication center of the production company at that point. He or she gets all the information possible from the crew and cast and disburses it to those who can use the information as efficiently as possible. An A.D.'s antennae must be long for that reason. If the First A.D. must leave the set for a few minutes, he or she always tells the crew in the immediate area and gives control of the set to the Second A.D., who will stand in for him or her, and likewise will not leave the camera area until relieved by the First A.D. This procedure is absolutely necessary because the crew must have someone to whom to turn for information, and who is feeding them the proper information at a moment's notice.

2104   Key Second Assistant Director

The Key Second A.D. is the right arm of the First A.D. The First cannot leave the set under normal circumstances, and can not leave the Director alone on the set. So when someone at the Honeywagons must call the actors out of makeup for rehearsal the task falls to the Key Second A.D. The Key Second A.D. also is responsible for the set paperwork, which is monumental. It encompasses the call sheet, production report, and SAG report, among other things.

> **Call Sheet**:   A rundown of tomorrow's activities, including times to report for work for crew and actors, what scenes are to be shot, and what requirements are necessary.
>
> **Production Report**:   Report of what happened during the day's work, which scenes were shot, how much film was used, how many pages were completed, and how many lunches were eaten.
>
> *SAG* **Report**:   A legal form filled out to send to the Screen Actors Guild giving the actors times in, times out, lunches, and so forth.

I always try to hire Second A.D.s who are capable of handling the job of First A.D. if necessary. My criterion always has been this: if I cannot do the job, the Second A.D. should be able to step over my body, pick up the book, and start shooting where I left off.

2105   Second Second Assistant Director

A Second Second A.D. usually is hired to help when vast numbers of extras are called, or when the Key Second A.D. is suffering from burnout. In days of yore we hired Production Assistants to help the Second A.D.s, but in modern times we have taken to hiring more and more Second A.D.s. On larger projects there is always a Second Second hired for the length of the show.

Second Second A.D.s also have the thankless job of filling out all the proper paperwork and giving it to the Key Second A.D. to give to the First A.D. Sometimes when huge numbers of extras are called, we will want to hire:

2106 Other Second Assistants
These folks just come in for a daily rate and do not work steadily on our picture.

2107 DGA Trainee
The DGA Training Program is managed jointly by the Directors Guild and the Producers Association. Its purpose is to feed a constant stream of well-trained, highly qualified production personnel into the business. That education takes the form of on-the-job training; DGA Trainees work on every conceivable type of production from major features to music videos to commercials. This is enhanced by weekly seminars that give the trainee valuable knowledge of safety rules, union restrictions, and such. DGA Trainees can be invaluable in helping with paperwork, helping to wrangle extras, and so forth.

2108 Production Associates
This euphemism for "Production Assistant" covers gofors. I have paid as little as $250 a week and as much as $500 for these P.A.s. A good P.A. can be worth a great deal and save the company thousands of dollars at times.

2109 Technical Advisor
When a project has specific problems, a technical advisor is absolutely invaluable in keeping the small, insignificant, but oh so important details from getting away from you. In *War and Remembrance* our tech was a marvelously knowledgeable retired U.S. Navy Captain named Dale Patterson, who knew protocol backward and forward and was able to obtain Navy cooperation in the use of Naval vessels in filming when necessary. He also kept us straight when it came to the proper way to wear insignia and ribbons. Not important, we say? No Navy person wants to see the Submarine Service Dolphins pinned on the actor's chest below the battle ribbons.

On *Police Story*, a Columbia Pictures Television Production, each episode was the story of a different police officer and how he or she solved a case. The officer whose story it was acted as our tech advisor for each show.

2110 Production Office Coordinator
The Production Office Coordinator (P.O.C.) runs the production office. We formerly referred to them as *Production Secretaries*. The job is extremely

important as the P.O.C. is the main record keeper for the company. Should there be an accident on the set, our P.O.C. will have kept all the records of the safety meetings and the training papers, and so forth, that will let OSHA know that we did everything possible to protect the crew. The P.O.C. keeps the paperwork flowing properly as well as being able to do various office tasks without having to be prompted, including setting up an office from scratch.

The P.O.C. usually gets plenty of prep time as well as the same amount of wrap time as the UPM.

2111 Assistant P.O.C.
The Assistant P.O.C. usually starts when the work load becomes too heavy for the P.O.C., sometimes a few weeks prior to filming. The job of P.O.C. is huge, on larger films far more than one person can handle.

2112 Local Production Office Coordinator
When we are on a distant location we will hire a local assistant for our P.O.C. who knows how to find the best deals are on that turf for office supplies, and the local customs for setting up a production office

2113 Script Supervisor

Description	Amount	Units	X	Rate	Subtotal
Prep	0	Week	1	1,416.73	0
Shoot	4	Weeks	1	1,416.73	5,667
Wrap	0	Week	1	1,416.73	0
					5,667
Overtime allowance	10	%	1	0	0
Personal Equipment Rental	10	Weeks	1	0	0
Car Allowance	0	Week	1	0	0
Computer Rental	0	Week	1	0	0
Script Timing	0	Flat	1	500	0
Multiple Camera Allowance	0	Allow	1	0	0
Polaroid Film/Camera	1	Allow	1	0	0
Total					**5,667**

The Script Supervisor is the eyes and ears of the Editor on the set. He or she keeps records of every shot, every take, what lens was used, how long the shot was in seconds and film feet, which magazine and film roll was used, in case the lab goofs up, and why the take was printed or not printed. All this information is necessary for the camera crew and sound crew. The script supervisor also is the final authority as to scene numbers; prior to each take, the sound and camera crews check with him or her as to what numbers appear on the "slate."

Continuity

One of the more important duties of the Script Supervisor is *continuity*, which is the preservation of uniformity from one shot to the next in a sequence. A simple example would be the length of a cigarette. Suppose we have filmed a master sequence in which one of our characters is just finishing a cigarette, and it is a stub. Then, we break for lunch before the close-ups. When we return from lunch we film close-ups of the same character for the same sequence, but this time the Actor has taken a new, full-length cigarette and is smoking it in the close-up. When the editor cuts from master to close-up and back, the cigarette will magically grow and shrink. Our Script Supervisor's job is to prevent that from happening.

Polaroid Camera and Film

Instant snapshots are becoming more and more prevalent as a means of keeping items consistent from one shot to the next. We will find a similar need in the Props, Wardrobe, and Makeup departments, where one needs to preserve continuity between shots.

2114 Production Accountant

Description	Amount	Units	X	Rate	Subtotal
Prep	0	Week	1	1,928.14	0
Shoot	4	Weeks	1	1,928.14	7,713
Wrap	0	Week	1	1,928.14	0
					7,713
Overtime allowance	10	%	1	0	0
Personal Equipment Rental	10	Weeks	1	0	0
Car Allowance	0	Week	1	0	0
Computer Rental	0	Week	1	0	0
Computer Supplies	0	Week	1	0	0
Total					**7,713**

The Production Accountant, also known as Production Auditor, could be a person or a company. Several good, well respected companies do production accounting, and many free-lance production accountants can use the numerous computer accounting programs on the market. In either case, the job is absolutely necessary. Someone has to pay the bills!

The Production Accountant normally begins working soon after the UPM joins the company, because bills start coming in shortly after that, such as bills for office rental and furniture, and bank accounts have to be set up. At the end of filming the Accountant usually stays on for as long as the UPM to finish paying all the bills that come in after the show has wrapped.

2115   Assistant Production Accountant

As the prep time closes in on the first day of filming, the Production Accountant will find that this job is far too much for one person to handle. An assistant usually joins the company a week or two prior to filming, and more often than not the job entails data entry into the accounting program. Therefore, the assistant has to be familiar with the accounting packages and usually knows something about computers as well.

2116   Payroll Secretary

The job of Payroll Secretary is almost a lost art by now. Most producers prefer to use payroll firms, because they are so facile. Today a Payroll Clerk is a little like a Stegosaurus. However, if the company still does its budgets on an abacus then by all means hire one.

2117   Local Auditor

On distant location, we will want to hire a local auditor to help with the books in that location. This person should know the local banking laws well and ideally should have a relationship with a local bank that will enable the company to open accounts locally and pay the local bills from it.

2118   Location Manager

The Location Manager finds locations, gets permission to film there, scours the surrounding neighborhood for unruly barking dogs, arranges a place for crew and trucks to park, arranges street use permits from local authorities, and often acts as the scapegoat when things entirely beyond anyone's control go awry.

It is a very large and important job, and great care must be taken to find the right person to do it. Often this job entails work at odd hours. If we wish to film in Beverly Hills, for instance, the Location Manager must canvass an area four square blocks around the filming location and obtain signatures from all the residents giving permission to film. Without the signatures the city won't give us a permit. So the Location Manager must be a diplomat as well as a logistical genius. For every location we must have plenty of parking space, room to feed the crew lunch, and convenient access for our trucks.

Normally the Location Manager would be listed in the Location Account; however I have put the Location Manager in the Production account because clearing locations is properly a production function. To confuse the issue even further, Location Managers are covered by the Teamsters Contract.

Notice that the Location Manager, per the Teamsters contract, gets *both* mileage allowance and car rental.

2119   Assistant Location Manager

While shooting is in progress, very often the Location Manager will have to leave the set to obtain the permits for the following day's work. Someone on the set has to handle the permits, so when the local police try to shoo us away we can prove that we have a legitimate right. Or, if we are on the street in front of a line of stores, someone can deal with the store owners, if it has not already been done. The A.D.s are too busy to handle that job, so an Assistant Location Manager is necessary.

Movie Magic Budgeting [BUDBOOK.MMB 2100 Production Staff]			
File Edit Setup Tools Library Go To Magic Window Help			
BUDBOOK.MMB 2,671,976 Category 2100 180,641	TOP SHEET ACCOUNT DETAIL	Cume: Change:	0 0

Acct#	Account Title	Page	Total
2119	Ass't Location Mgr	11	2,964
2120	Interpreters	11	0
2121	Government Rep.	11	0
2122	Censor	11	0
2123	Safety Officers	12	12,000
2124	Production Board/Budget	12	0
2125	Office Expenses	12	0
2197	Loss & Damage	12	0
2198	Miscellaneous	12	630
2199	**Total Fringes**		**40,569**
	Total		**180,641**

2120-21-22   Interpreter, Government Representative, Censor

These folks only will be assigned to our film when it is filmed in a foreign country, and then not very often.

Of course, if we are filming in a foreign country where the native tongue is not English, we will have to communicate to the crew somehow. Then an interpreter is necessary, although a bilingual Assistant Director can be invaluable. When I filmed *Bananas* in Puerto Rico, I learned some Hispanic movie terms. When we rolled the camera the A.D. would yell, "El Rollo!" When the camera ran out of film it was, "El Reloado."

2123 Safety Officer

MMB	Movie Magic Budgeting - [BUDBOOK.MMB — 2123 — Safety Officers]					_ ▯ X	
MMB	File Edit Setup Tools Library Go To Magic Window Help					_ ▯ X	
BUDBOOK.MMB	2,671,976		TOP SHEET		Cume:	0	
Category 2100	180,641		ACCOUNT		Change:	0	
Account 2123	12,000		DETAIL				

Description	Amount	Units	X	Rate	Subtotal
Safety Officer:	0		1	0	0
Prep	0	Week	1	1,200	0
Shoot	10	Weeks	1	1,200	12,000
Wrap	0	Week	1	1,200	0
					12,000
Assistants:	0		1	0	0
Prep	0	Week	1	750	0
Shoot	0	Week	1	750	0
Wrap	0	Week	1	750	0
					0
Overtime allowance	10	%	1	0	0
Total					**12,000**

By now the subject of set safety has assumed such overriding importance that most major studios and large independent producers employ a person whose only function on the set is to keep straight the safety paperwork, videotape the rehearsals and safety meetings, etc.

Safety on the Set

In production the Assistant Director is the official head of all safety operations on the set. The A.D. is responsible for working with the Stunt Gaffer and the Special Effects crew, giving them the time to prepare their stunts and effects thoroughly and safely.

In California a law, SB 198, states very clearly that the employer is responsible for making the set at safe as humanly possible. This means:

1. Upon being hired, a crew person by law must be given a written booklet outlining all the safety rules of the company, as well as maps showing all the safety exits of the workplace. This is the law, not tradition. Each member of the crew must acknowledge receiving the safety pamphlet by signing a receipt for it, and those receipts must be kept in the office by the P.O.C. or on set by the Safety Officer.

2. When a stunt or effect is to take place a safety meeting must be called in which the action is explained to at least all the heads of departments and any crew people directly involved. A sheet must be passed around that everyone signs to prove that there was a safety meeting. A map must be drawn up showing where the event is to take place, particularly where the crew can stand out of harm's way. Each member of the crew must have that map.

3. Prior to each event, the stunt or effect must be rehearsed, in slow motion when possible. Every member of the cast and crew who rehearses must sign a sheet affirming his or her presence at the rehearsal. Many

companies have handi-cams on the set to photograph these rehearsals in detail to prove that they happened. The purpose of all this is that if, God forbid, an accident causes either dismemberment (a crew member loses the tip of a finger) or unconsciousness, by law Office of Safety and Health Administration (OSHA) must investigate. If the investigation shows that the employer did not follow standard procedure with rehearsals, safety meetings, and so on, the company is fined *very* heavily and sometimes shut down. So these meetings, maps, and pamphlets are important proof that the employer has been mindful of the safety of the employees.

4. One more thing, when each member of the crew is employed, the employer must verify that the person knows how to use all the tools available to the craft. This verification may be done with a diploma or certificate showing that the crew member has been trained in the use of the tools. A copy of that certificate must be kept on file along with all the other safety-related papers. If the crew member has had no formal training, the employer must give the employee a lesson in how to use the tools and then may give the crew member the certificate of training for the employee's records. But each employee must have such a certificate. If the crew member belongs to a union, membership in the union is sufficient to show that the person is adept at using the tools of that department.

2200 Art Direction

Acct#	Account Title	Page	Total
2201	Production Designer	12	10,000
2202	Art Director	13	22,235
2203	Assistant Art Director	13	6,657
2204	Set Designer	13	5,144
2205	Draftsman	13	0
2206	Graphic Designer	13	0
2207	Sketch Artist	13	0
2208	Storyboard Artist	13	0
2209	Models	13	0
2210	Set Estimator	14	0
2211	Blueprints	14	0
2212	Materials & Supplies	14	0
2213	Office Costs	14	0
2214	Secretaries	14	10,000
2297	Loss & Damage	14	0
2298	Miscellaneous	14	0
2299	**Total Fringes**		17,164
	Total		71,200

The Art Department is responsible for seeing that all the movie's visual elements work together properly. This includes color, tone, feel, wardrobe, sets, and textures – everything.

Our job is to sell a film as real. Our audience must believe that those people on the screen are living, breathing creatures with whom they can empathize. Any element that reminds the audience that it is sitting in a theater watching a show is jarring. It destroys the reality of the piece. That element can be something as unobtrusive as a Roman Legionnaire wearing a Seiko digital wristwatch, or as gross as a movie I saw once in which John Dillinger made his getaway from a bank robbery in a 1951 Buick.

Almost everyone in this department needs considerable prep, but no wrap is necessary. The Art Director can put his or her pencils in a pocket and leave on the last day of filming.

2201 Production Designer

Description	Amount	Units	X	Rate	Subtotal
Prep	0	Week	1	2,500	0
Shoot	4	Weeks	1	2,500	10,000
					10,000
Overtime allowance	10	%	1	0	0
Personal Equipment Rental	10	Weeks	1	0	0
Car Allowance	0	Week	1	0	0
Total					**10,000**

(Movie Magic Budgeting - [BUDBOOK.MMB - 2201 - Production Designer]; BUDBOOK.MMB 2,671,976; Category 2200 71,200; Account 2201 10,000)

The "Look" of a picture is very important. The visual elements must have some unity. The Production Designer's job is to keep that unity from being invaded by anachronism or other distractions.

The Production Designer helps to determine the "look" of the picture. A good Production Designer will add immeasurably to the production, and save countless thousands of dollars as well.

By the way, the reverse also is true. On a show at a major studio a few years back, we were scheduled to film on Stage 5 in the morning and move to an interior yacht set on Stage 4 just before lunch. While the shot was being lit on Stage 5, I walked next door into Stage 4. Surprise! No set was there! I quickly asked the Production Designer where he had been building the yacht. "What yacht?" I ran to the schedule only to find that nothing else could be filmed that day. Needless to say, the entire crew stood around for four hours with nothing to film while the set was being constructed.

Sometimes a Production Designer will use a computer to generate graphics of the sets being designed. In that case, we will rent the Designer's computer from him because one can't rent a computer with Art Director programs already installed.

2202 Art Director
Sometimes the person in charge of the "look" of the film is called the "Art Director" and no "Production Designer" is on the staff. Some films have both. I did a very large picture several years ago that called for sets in several places at once on a distant location. The Production Designer was in charge of the overall look of the picture, and each location had its own Art Director who was in charge of that particular location.

2204 Set Designer
If we are lucky, our production designer will draw all renderings plus elevations and overheads. If not, the Set Designer draws those.

2205   Draftsman
The Draftsman does pretty much the same thing as the Set Designer but in greater detail and can produce blueprints.

2206   Graphic Designer
Sometimes the company needs a special item to be designed, such as a futuristic underwater show involving the use of whiz-bang scuba gear. A Graphic Designer would be used to design the scuba gear. The legendary Ralph McQuarrie, one of the best Graphic Designers, designed most of the machinery for the *Star Wars* trilogy.

2207   Sketch Artist
Sometimes the Production Designer cannot draw at all. Then, we need someone to do the drawings. These are not the mechanical drawings from which the sets are to be constructed, but the renderings to give the Director and Producer an idea of what the sets will look like.

2208   Storyboard Artist
This is a duplicate of Account 1506. Some Producers prefer to keep all the artists in the Art Department.

2209   Models
At times a Director will want models of the sets to better envision the camera angles. These are little cardboard-cutout sets with all the doorways and windows in the right places. The Director can use little stick-figure models to walk from room to room, even have a little camera on a tiny tripod to help get the angles down. This is one place where that could go in the budget. It also might go under Set Construction and Miniature work.

2210   Set Estimator
Someone has to estimate how much it will cost to build the sets. Usually the Art Director will do this, but on exceptionally large projects a set estimator may be employed. On *War and Remembrance* we had an excellent set estimator who carried one of those bicycle wheels on a long pole attached to an odometer. He could estimate the board-footage of a set to within a couple percent.

2211   Blueprints
If we need blueprints, we need to have them made somewhere, in addition to just being designed, as in Account 2205.

2212   Materials and Supplies
Artists must have paper and pencils to do their work.

2214 Secretaries

So many people worked in the Art Department on *War and Remembrance* that it had its own phone lines, secretary, and reception area. I cannot imagine that a secretary would be necessary on an average picture, but then what picture is average these days?

2297 Loss and Damage

The picture will need to buy insurance against the possibility of loss or damage due to accidents or acts of God. This insurance usually has a "deductible" amount. We put that deductible amount in the "Loss and Damage" field in each account where it could apply.

2300 Set Construction

Acct#	Account Title	Page	Total
2301	Construction Coordinator	15	20,500
2302	Construction Foreman	15	0
2303	Construction Labor	15	0
2304	Construction Materials	15	0
2305	Paint Department	15	0
2306	Carpenters	15	0
2307	Plumbers	16	0
2308	Electrical Fixtures Men	16	0
2309	Plasterers	16	0
2310	Labor Department	16	0
2311	First Aid	16	0
2312	Watchmen/Security	16	0
2313	Construction Space	16	0
2314	Tools	16	0
2315	Office Expenses	17	0
2316	Backings	17	0
2317	Trash Removal	17	0
2318	Construction Vehicles	17	0
2319	Special Equipment	17	0
2320	Scaffolding	17	0

Sets can be constructed in several ways. To begin with, we must determine if we want to construct sets or if it would be more cost-effective to film on location. Balance off the cost of studio rental (or space rental, if renting a warehouse) and set construction against the cost of location rental and refurbishment, then dial in the location equipment costs and extra personnel, drivers, and so forth.

After that, we can either hire our own set construction crew, headed up by our own construction coordinator, rent tools, and so on, or hire a set construction company to build sets for us as an all-in package. Be sure the company's bid includes striking and disposing of the set!

2301 Construction Coordinator

Description	Amount	Units	X	Rate	Subtotal
Prep	0	Week	1	1,750	0
Shoot	4	Weeks	1	1,750	7,000
Wrap	0	Weeks	1	1,750	0
Prep Distant	0	DistWks	1	2,250	0
Shoot Distant	6	DistWks	1	2,250	13,500
Wrap Distant	0	DistWks	1	2,250	0
					20,500
Overtime allowance	10	%	1	0	0
Tool rental	0	Weeks	1	0	0
Shop Rental	0	Week	1	0	0
Car Allowance	0	Week	1	0	0
Total					**20,500**

This is the construction gang boss. This person will hire a proper crew and oversee all phases of set construction. Most Construction Coordinators rent their own tools to us at a considerable savings over what we would have spent at E-Z Rentals down the street. The Construction Coordinator may also have a "mill" or set-construction shop we can lease in which to build our sets.

2302 Construction Foreman
One level down from the Construction Coordinator, the construction foreman normally is in charge of just one location. If our film involves construction on several locations simultaneously we will hire a foreman for each.

2303 Construction Labor
It is not unusual for lower budget productions to subcontract the set construction to a construction company specializing in building sets. We have to be careful to get references and check them out for financial reliability as well as expertise in set construction before we take such a step.

2311 First Aid
Because of SB 198, almost all productions keep a medic on-site at all filming and construction sites. Medics help in little ways every day and are there in case of emergency. They also have the names and phone numbers of the hospitals nearest the site, a legal requirement now.

When we have no Medic on site is when things happen. Sometimes when a Medic is on site things happen anyway. When we were constructing the White House interiors for *War and Remembrance* a carpenter fell through the ceiling of the set and dropped about 20 feet to the floor below, severely dislocating his gazotskis and shattering his frammis in the process. Thank goodness the Medic took charge, immediately applied some Oil of

Sea-Slug or something, and had the man transported to the local emergency ward.

2312 Watchman

For the same show we had to construct the White House rear portico on the parking lot of the warehouse we rented for the Roosevelt and Churchill Christmas scene. A few of the locals were covetous of White House memorabilia, especially prior to our filming it, and our Watchman certainly earned his keep for those few days.

2316 Backings

> **Backings and Translights**: Those huge paintings which appear outside of windows on stage to emulate the New York skyline or the Grand Canyon, when we can't afford to go there on location. These can be rented from such places as J.C. Backings. Making them yourself is a tedious process and not very rewarding. Translights are the same for night scenes; the windows have translucent cutouts through which a soft light can shine, emulating lit windows.

2317 Trash removal

You would be surprised how this item can jump up and bite us in the neck if we haven't provided for it. The EPA now has laws about disposal of paint, wood, and other set construction materials. After filming, we must return the location to the condition in which we found it. If we have half-filled paint cans we must give them over to one of the several paint disposal companies in the area or else have the hazardous material folks handle them.

2322 Models

This seems like a duplication, doesn't it? Actually, some companies prefer to assign budget items to one account and some to another. So we will find some apparent duplication scattered throughout this budget form.

2323 Miniatures

Sometimes it pays to use miniatures rather than build entire sets. In *War and Remembrance* we needed to photograph the south façade of the White House but we didn't want to transport the crew and cast to Washington DC just for one shot, so we had the Art Director construct a perfect replica of the White House. We photographed it against a grassy field in San Fernando. It was only about 6 feet tall and 10 feet wide, but it was so well built that with the false perspective of our photography it appeared that our extras were actually walking back and forth a couple of hundred yards away from the White House itself.

2323   Construction Package
If we are soliciting bids for the construction package, this account is where the bids should be entered.

2397   Loss and Damage
The insurance deductible figure goes here as always.

2400 Set Decoration

Acct#	Account Title	Page	Total
2401	Set Decorator	18	7,848
2402	Lead Man	18	7,381
2403	Swing Gang	18	19,253
2404	Extra Men	18	0
2405	Local Labor	18	0
2406	Draper	18	6,418
2407	Drapery	19	0
2408	Carpet Man	19	19,253
2409	Carpets	19	0
2410	Fixture Man	19	19,253
2411	Fixtures	19	0
2412	Greensmen	19	19,253
2413	Greens	19	0
2414	Dressings Purchased	19	0
2415	Dressing Rentals	19	0
2416	Office Expenses	19	0
2497	Loss & Damage	20	0
2498	Miscellaneous	20	0
2499	**Total Fringes**		**26,360**
	Total		125,019

In very broad terms the "Set Decorators" or "Set Dressers" are persons who put into the sets those items, such as the furniture and accoutrements, which will be sat on, eaten off, or otherwise used in the scene by the performers during the shoot. These are not properties – that's another item. Easy way to remember the difference: if an Actor sits on a chair it is set dressing. If the Actor throws the chair at another Actor it is a prop.

2401 Set Decorator

Description	Amount	Units	X	Rate	Subtotal
Prep	0	Week	1	1,962.10	0
Shoot	4	Weeks	1	1,962.10	7,848
Wrap	0	Week	1	1,962.10	0
					7,848
Overtime allowance	10	%	1	0	0
Personal Equipment Rental	10	Weeks	1	0	0
Car Allowance	10	Weeks	1	0	0
Total					7,848

A Set Decorator must work in very close contact with the Production Designer. We don't want to have a Greek Revival house stocked with Louis XIV furniture – or maybe we do. Come to think of it, that would be an amusing combination.

Also please note that we haven't yet added Prep or Wrap for our decorator, who will need both. If we don't give the Decorator enough time to prep the show, we won't have any furniture for the sets on the first day of filming. The job entails not just hauling the furniture from the rental house to the set and back, but also choosing what furniture to use, so the time will be well spent. I usually try to hire the Set Decorator very shortly after hiring the Art Director, who also has the prerogative of input regarding whom to hire as Set Decorator. They do have to work together, after all.

After filming is completed the set dressing crew will need a few days to return the furniture and so on to the rental houses. A member of the set dressing crew should always be there for the check-in, so that the rental house can give our employee the receipt for everything returned and consequently be prevented from billing us (in error, of course) for items we returned but they claim we did not.

2402 Lead Man
The Set Decorator generally has a crew to help carry the furniture and other items about. This crew is known as the *Swing Gang*. The foreman of the swing gang is known as the *Lead Man*. Usually heavier pictures could have five or six on the Swing Gang in addition to the Lead Man. And depending on the amount and size of the items being used, they will need enough time to bring the dressing to the sets and return them to the rental houses.

2404 Extra Workers
Sometimes when the going gets rough we will need extra workers to help out for a day or so. This is true not only in the Set Decoration department but in all departments.

2406 Draper
The Draper hangs the window curtains. Generally anything that hangs and is fabric is handled by the Draper. In the case of *Hamlet* the arrass is handled by the Draper.

2408 Carpet Man
The Carpet Man is the person who puts things of fabric on the floor to be trod on.

2410 Fixture Man
Fixtures are things that hang from the walls or ceilings and contain things that give off light. A Fixture Man takes care of placing them, but an electrician must hook them to some power if they require electricity.

2412 Greensman

Very often we will need things which are green and have some part of their being planted in the ground. The Greensman places and cares for these plants. Several very good greens rental houses in Los Angeles cater specifically to the movie industry.

2414-15 Dressing Purchased and Rented

We have to be careful not to make the mistake of so many first-time budgeters – to budget for personnel but not for set dressing materials. If we have no materials we will have no furniture in our sets.

2500 Property Department

Acct#	Account Title	Page	Total
2501	Property Master	20	7,848
2502	Assistant Prop Master	20	7,381
2503	Buyer	20	6,418
2504	Local Hire	20	6,418
2505	Rentals	21	0
2506	Purchases	21	0
2507	Manufactures	21	0
2508	Animals	21	0
2509	Picture Vehicles	21	0
2510	Armorer	21	0
2511	Firearms	21	0
2512	Video Playback System	21	0
2513	Office Expenses	21	0
2514	Box Rentals	21	2,000
2597	Loss & Damage	21	0
2598	Miscellaneous	21	0
2599	**Total Fringes**		9,395
	Total		39,460

> **Properties**: Items held by the actors or used by them somehow in the telling of the story. Pistols which shoot are properties. Pistols displayed on the wall are Set Dressing.

Like the Set Decorators, the Property Department people need time to prepare and wrap a show. And they need time prior to filming to show the important props to the Director for approval. And, if the Director needs to have props replaced, there must be time prior to filming for replacement.

Likewise, the Property folks need time after shooting is finished to return the props to the prop rental houses. It's cheap insurance against the property rental house trying to charge us for props not returned, which really were.

2501 Property Master

Description	Amount	Units	X	Rate	Subtotal
Prep	0	Week	1	1,962.10	0
Shoot	4	Weeks	1	1,962.10	7,848
Wrap	0	Week	1	1,962.10	0
					7,848
Overtime allowance	10	%	1	0	0
Personal Equipment Rental	10	Weeks	1	0	0
Car Allowance	10	Weeks	1	0	0
Total					7,848

The Property Master works independently from the Art Department, but normally defers to the taste of the Production Designer in choice of Props.

A Note on Production Procedure

I have found it extremely useful to set aside a few minutes each day during pre-production for department heads to get together for an informal production meeting. Not mandatory, only those who happen to be in the office, and the Director usually is present as well. If department heads are not available they generally have their second in command appear.

The purpose is for people to discuss mutual problems affecting more than one department in the presence of the Director, whose taste controls the artistic side of the picture. I usually arrange these meetings around 9:00 AM or 5:00 PM, and they usually last around 10-15 minutes. Doing so sometimes (but not always) prevents Set Decorators and Property Masters from renting identical objects when each thinks he or she is responsible for that object. But most importantly it urges people to talk to each other and work problems out together.

2502   Assistant Property Master
Usually spends a week or two less on prep than the Property Master himself and helps with the wrap. The assistant always stays on set, in case the Prop Master has to run out for a prop which is missing or which suddenly becomes essential.

2503   Buyer
Sometimes time restrictions make it impossible for the Property Master to shop for everything, so a Buyer will be hired to do some of the shopping.

2504   Local Hires
Once again, if filming on distant location, we may need the help of a local who knows where to find the best stores and the best prices.

2508 Animals

Description	Amount	Units	X	Rate	Subtotal	
Wrangler	0		1	0	0	
Prep	0		1	0	0	
Shoot	0		1	0	0	
Additional Wranglers	0		1	0	0	
Animal Handlers	0		1	0	0	
Training	0		1	0	0	
Animal Rental	0		1	0	0	
Transport	0		1	0	0	
Food	0		1	0	0	
Kennel/Stable/Cage/Box	0		1	0	0	
Total					**0**	

(Window header: *Horse Magic* Budgeting - [BUDBOOK.MMB - 2508 - Animals])
(File Edit Setup Tools Library Go To Magic Window Help)
BUDBOOK.MMB 2,671,976
Category 2500 39,460
Account 2508 0
Cume: 0
Change: 0

Animals have long been the purview of the Teamsters Union. The word *Teamster* derives from those men who drove the "Teams" of horses or oxen on wagons such as covered wagons, most of which, by the way, were manufactured by the Studebaker Company.

Two major items become involved when we need to use animals in our show: maintenance and the ASPCA.

Maintenance

Animals must be tended by wranglers. Animals also need food, shelter, transport, and whatever else is necessary to stay healthy and happy. An experienced wrangler will be able to help us with that. See the preceding chart for all the possibilities.

The ASPCA

The American Society for the Prevention of Cruelty to Animals must be notified whenever an animal will be used in the picture. The law is very clear about our use of animals.

> **Animal Law**: In short, no animal may be harmed or even discomforted in any way for the sake of a picture. The ASPCA will assign an officer to our set to ensure that animals are treated properly, if there is even a hint of animal abuse in the script.

2509 Picture Vehicles

A much larger account appears in the Transportation Category, Account 3606, dealing with Picture Vehicles. If we have only one or two of them they could be listed here. And some producers prefer to have the picture vehicles budgeted into the Property account.

I remember working on a TV show that had a truck completely rigged with exploding bumpers, twirling hubcaps, and the like. The truck's construction was overseen jointly by the Transportation Department, Props, and Special Effects, and we had to have a special "truck meeting" every day to monitor its progress.

2510-11 Firearms and Blanks

If we have gunshots of any kind, by law, a crew member with a powder license must handle the firearms for us. Very strict laws govern the use of firearms and explosives of all kinds, and these must be strictly adhered to. At times the presence of fire safety officers and paramedics may be necessary. Our permit will require it.

Firearm Safety

Whenever working with firearms of any kind on the set, we need to take several precautions:

1.   The local authorities must be notified well beforehand and all necessary permits must be obtained.

2.   The crew must attend the mandatory safety meeting and be given the mandatory area map. The map must include the name and telephone number of the closest hospital just in case anything untoward happens.

3.   The crew, and any nearby cast, must be given ear protectors. Even quarter-load blanks are loud.

4.   If the gun will be pointed toward the camera the camera crew must be protected behind a plexiglass shield.

5.   The rest of the crew must be kept well enough away from the shooting that they could not possibly be injured by stray blank wadding, and that their ears cannot be hurt by the noise.

6.   The Assistant Director, the de facto safety officer on the set, must make sure every precaution has been taken to protect the crew, cast, and bystanders before commencing the filming. Then just prior to rolling sound and camera, the A.D. should announce loudly to all, "Gunshots!"

2512 Video Playback System

This is used when we have an Actor watching TV on screen. For that to happen on camera, we need a method of synching the VCR to the camera at 24 frames. Several good companies in Hollywood specialize in just that.

Also, if what the character is seeing on TV is anything other than stock footage, we probably will have to film it ourselves. To enable it to be shown on camera, when we schedule the film, we will have to schedule that scene which appears on the TV set to be filmed first, and allow plenty of time for processing.

2513 Box Rentals

Every property master has a huge box filled with props of all kinds to rent to us for the picture. We would be wise to take it. It will save our tails more than once when the Director decides to use a prop he or she forgot to tell anyone about prior to filming.

2597 Loss and Damage

When a rented item in any category is lost or damaged, the production company will have to repair or replace it. This was true on a well known, very expensive commercial flop, which used real antique rifles during the battle scenes. Many of these priceless gems were ruined or destroyed during the filming. Their loss and damage bill was enough to pay for a few little movies in itself.

2600 Camera Operations

Acct#	Account Title	Page	Total
2601	Director of Photography	22	20,000
2602	Operator	22	11,222
2603	1st Assistant Camera	22	12,241
2604	2nd Assistant Camera	22	9,965
2605	Extra Operator	22	0
2606	Extra Assistants	22	0
2607	Extra Loader	23	0
2608	Steadicam Operator	23	0
2609	Steadicam Equipment	23	0
2610	Standby D.P.	23	0
2611	Camera Package	23	125,000
2612	Special Rentals	23	0
2613	Purchases	23	0
2614	Video Assist	23	0
2615	Stillsman	23	9,741
2616	Still Equipment	24	0
2617	Shipping & Handling	24	0
2618	Process Department	24	0
2697	Loss & Damage	24	0
2698	Miscellaneous	24	0

Movie Magic Budgeting - [BUDBOOK.MMB -- 2600 -- Camera Operations]
File Edit Setup Tools Library Go To Magic Window Help
BUDBOOK.MMB 2,671,976 Category 2600 203,446
Cume: 0 Change: 0

In movies and TV, another character is always on stage with the actors: the camera. The camera has a definite point of view. The Director's job is to make that point of view a cohesive part of the picture. The Director therefore chooses the point of view the audience should take for each shot. The Cinematographer, or Director of Photography, lights and composes each shot according to the Director's wishes in the most artistic, effective way.

2601 Director of Photography

Movie Magic Budgeting - [BUDBOOK.MMB -- 2601 -- Director of Photography]
File Edit Setup Tools Library Go To Magic Window Help
BUDBOOK.MMB 2,672,212 Category 2600 203,446 Account 2601 20,000
Cume: 0 Change: 0

Description	Amount	Units	X	Rate	Subtotal
Prep	0	Week	1	5,000	0
Shoot	4	Weeks	1	5,000	20,000
					20,000
Kit Rental	10	Weeks	1	0	0
Total					20,000

The Director of Photography (D.P.) makes the camera and lighting decisions. He or she brings years of experience to bear on the problems posed by the Director.

In the early days of film Cameramen needed little talent beyond the ability to turn the crank at an even speed. All movies were filmed outdoors; even the interiors were filmed in roofless stages. So lighting was no problem; turning that crank was.

Today the D.P. is a key member of the creative team. A good D.P. can make a film better by suggesting angles and lighting themes to the Director.

The D.P. needs enough prep to visit the locations or sets and determine the lighting and camera equipment necessary to film properly. Usually the Chief Lighting Technician and Key Grip will accompany the D.P. on any scout, and will aid in the discussion of equipment needs. The D.P. generally needs no wrap at all. But when the film is being timed in the lab, the D.P. usually is present for that process.

2602 Camera Operator

The Camera Operator physically runs the camera, making sure the pans are smooth, and so forth. In smaller productions, very low budget films and the like, the camera crew might consist of only two people, a D.P./Operator and an Assistant. The Camera Operator needs neither prep nor wrap, only shoot time.

2603 First Assistant Cameraman

In England the First Assistant Cameraman is known as the Focus Puller, whose job is to follow-focus (hence "Focus Puller"), set F-stops, change lenses, load the camera, and physically care for the camera. The Camera Operator has only two hands, and those are engaged in keeping the camera aimed properly. Therefore two extra hands are necessary to keep the focus exact and to handle the Zoom lens.

If the camera package is from Panavision, a Panaflex package or better, the Assistant must also be an experienced camera technician for which a higher rate is paid. We never know when the darn thing will fail. Inevitably it will be in the middle of the desert near Lake Mead with Panavision at least five hours away.

2604 Second Assistant Cameraman

This person loads the magazines, keeps the lenses clean, and in general trains to be a good Focus-Puller. Since the slate is also part of the Second A.C.'s responsibility, in England the term is "Clapper Boy." Another very important part of the Second A.C.'s job is to write the Scene and Take Numbers on the camera report which accompanies every roll of film. These numbers keep the camera and sound systems in sync.

2605 Extra Operator

If more than one camera works in any one shot, we will need people to handle that extra camera. If it's more than one or two shots, most likely we will hire an extra Operator and Camera Assistant to handle each extra camera for those shots.

2608-09   Steadicam or Panaglide Operator

Steadicam and Panaglide are camera stabilizing systems. Whenever a shot requires a handheld camera while the operator is running or going up or down stairs, for instance, the camera must be stabilized so that the picture will be steady no matter how much jerking around the operator is doing. This system requires special personnel to use it properly, usually someone with enough heft to have a low center of gravity. The systems are designed for hand-held operation and the harness the operator wears has various springs and shock absorbers which damp unwanted movements.

Steadicam equipment and operators usually are hired just for the days necessary and require no prep or wrap.

2611   Rentals

Description	Amount	Units	X	Rate	Subtotal
Basic Camera Package	10	Weeks	1	12,500	125,000
Extra Cameras	0	Day	1	0	0
Total					**125,000**

BUDBOOK.MMB 2,671,976 / Category 2600 203,446 / Account 2611 125,000 / Cume: 0 / Change: 0

Camera Package

Some Directors of Photography prefer a Panavision Package, others prefer Arriflex, and still others prefer more experimental systems such as Moviecam. Panavision generally is a shade more quiet than Arriflex, although the difference is noticeable only in a quiet neighborhood in Gunnison, CO, at 3:00 AM in the basement of a house on a cul-de-sac. Both cameras, over the years, have evolved to the point at which they are quiet and not horribly expensive. If we have an extremely low-budget film we may wish to consider 16mm. The print will have more grain than 35mm will, but then wouldn't life be dull without a little grain now and again?

Second Camera

When we rent a camera package more than likely a second camera body (without lenses) will be in the package. There also will be times when it is efficient to use both cameras at once, one filming the master scene and the other filming a close-up, or some similar combination. This arrangement saves time. However, this practice can boomerang when the two cameras are not placed properly and photograph each other.

Extra Camera Equipment

Description	Amount	Units	X	Rate	Subtotal
2nd Camera	0		1	0	0
Steadicam Package	0		1	0	0
Video Assist	0		1	0	0
Underwater Equipment	0		1	0	0
Aerial Cameras	0		1	0	0
Hi-Speed Cameras	0		1	0	0
Extra Cameras	0		1	0	0
Telephoto Lenses	0		1	0	0
Macro Lenses	0		1	0	0
Periscope Lenses	0		1	0	0
Telextenders	0		1	0	0
Remote Cameras	0		1	0	0
Stunt Cameras (Helmet)	0		1	0	0
Pogo-Cams	0		1	0	0
Extra Lenses	0		1	0	0
Special Cameras	0		1	0	0
Special Lenses	0		1	0	0
Total					**0**

The camera department can explain all these add-ons and accessories. A couple deserve mentioning in particular:

Underwater Cameras

If the script calls for underwater filming, we will probably hire someone like Jack Cooperman, A.S.C. He and other underwater specialists bring their own camera packages, which they maintain themselves and therefore are very reliable. They also will bring their assistants, who will be certified for underwater work.

Underwater Safety

This is very important. For underwater filming, we must be sure that any crew members participating are N.A.U.I or P.A.D.I. certified Scuba Divers and familiar with general safety requirements such as bottom time. Failure to do so could cost these people their lives. We also must hire a dive master or appoint one from the available certified crew. This person will be responsible for keeping air tanks filled and keeping track of crew bottom times, preventing the bends, and so forth.

Our underwater photographer will most likely make us a package deal for himself or herself, an assistant, and the camera equipment, and underwater lights and other necessary equipment. Also such companies as

Motion Picture Marine specialize in putting together an entire water package – boats, catering, accommodations – and generally act as water producer for the show.

Aerial Cameras

Aerial cameras usually are Tyler Mounts, although other companies, like Continental Camera, have excellent mounts for aerial work. Again, a number of companies and individuals can contract to rent an entire aerial package including the vehicle (plane or helicopter), camera mounts, camera package (which must be mated to the mount), pilot, camera assistant, gasoline truck, landing permits, and so on.

Hi-Speed Cameras

These can mean anything from a high-speed motor for a regular camera to an ultra-high-speed, 10,000 frames per second (fps) camera for special effects. Most cameras can be fitted with motors that will grind up to 128 fps. Anything higher usually requires special equipment such as a Waddell camera or special strobe lights. Remember that the faster the camera operates, the more light is necessary to light the subject due to the faster exposure time, more electricity is necessary to run the whole thing, and so forth.

Extra Cameras

Generally extra cameras are not necessary unless we are filming a very intricate and involved special effect or stunt or both. In that case, we may wish to rent four or more cameras to photograph the same action from different angles, because rebuilding the set we have just blown up for take 2 is very time consuming. I have even purchased a small camera to be inside a car while is being wrecked, knowing that the camera will be destroyed also, but praying that the film would come out all right.

Pogo-Cams

These ingenious devices help the operator balance a small camera, like an Eyemo, with counterweights and intended to be hand held. If we can't afford a Steadicam, we will try this.

2613 Purchases

The Camera department will have to purchase a number of items as our film progresses. Usually expendables, such as black bags, film cans, tape, chalk for the slate, cores, they will be purchased at very low cost from companies which specialize in selling these items.

2614   Video Assist

Description	Amount	Units	X	Rate	Subtotal
Camera Tap Rental	0		1	0	0
Monitor	0		1	0	0
Cassette Recorder	0		1	0	0
Cassette Purchases	0		1	0	0
Operator	0	Day	1	217.48	0
Extra Equipment	0		1	0	0
Total					0

Presently, there are two major forms of video assist systems and a plethora of companies that handle both quite well. Any camera rental firm will rent us a camera rigged with a video tap, which will enable the camera assistant to attach a small video camera to the film camera's reflex system. We can run a monitor off this, enabling the Director, D.P., and other crew members to watch the scene on the monitor through the camera lens. We can also use the second kind of video assist, which is to videotape each take and play it back later. This affords the Actors a chance to view their own performances and insist on another take, which is not very cost effective and therefore not recommended. Unless our Director is acting in a scene and must see the scene later, the latter system can cause far more harm than good; much time can be wasted.

2615-16   Still Photographer and Equipment

See also the comments under Publicity, Account 6304. Usually a Still Photographer on the set photographs everything from rehearsals to makeup, the Director chatting up the actors between takes, and similar scenes. Try to avoid the problem I had once. The network assigned a perfectly nice, artistic photographer to shoot stills who just happened to be stone deaf and couldn't hear the A.D. yell "Roll it." The unfortunate Photographer wandered into shots as they were being filmed, not knowing that the camera was rolling.

2618   Process Photography

Description	Amount	Units	X	Rate	Subtotal
Director of Photography	0		1	0	0
Assistant Camera	0		1	0	0
Electrical/Grip Crew	0		1	0	0
Grip Dept.	0		1	0	0
Matte Artist	0		1	0	0
Matte Crew	0		1	0	0
Location Travel/Hotel/Per Diem	0		1	0	0
Rear Screen	0		1	0	0
Front Screen	0		1	0	0
Mock Up	0		1	0	0
Rentals	0		1	0	0
Purchases	0		1	0	0
Raw Stock	0		1	0	0
Lab Fees	0		1	0	0
Synch System	0		1	0	0
Projection System	0		1	0	0
Projectionist	0		1	0	0
Total					**0**

We need two shots of our main character standing in front of the White House in Washington DC. The cost of transporting an entire crew to Washington just for the two shots is prohibitive. What to do? We need contemporary shots of the White House, and all the stock footage we have seen in at least two years old.

Process Photography is the answer. We phone a D.P. in Washington and ask for two shots, each 100 feet in length (That's over a minute, plenty of time for our shot). The film is sent to us the next day. We have it developed and now have two shots of the White House on *Background Plates*.

We set up a screen in front of our camera, and behind the screen we have a projector. That projector is projecting, from the rear, our picture of the White House. That's why this is often called *Rear Projection*. The Actor stands between the camera and screen, and both projector and camera are started simultaneously. Now we are photographing the Actor in front of a screen showing a movie of the White House, and it looks to our camera as if the Actor is in front of the White House. One more thing, we have to keep the projector and camera locked in synch, so we need a *Selsyn* system which connects the projector and camera mechanically so the shutters on both will open and shut simultaneously. See the Post-production area, Account 5609.

2700   Electric Operations

Acct#	Account Title	Page	Total
2701	Chief Lighting Technician	25	7,781
2702	Best Boy	25	7,034
2703	Electricians	25	20,160
2704	Extra Electricians	25	0
2705	Local Hires	25	0
2706	Generator Operator	25	7,034
2707	Pre-rig Crew	25	0
2708	Strike Crew	25	0
2709	Generator Rental	25	0
2710	Equipment Rentals	26	75,000
2711	Musco Lights	26	0
2712	Purchases	26	0
2713	Power charges	26	0
2797	Loss & Damage	26	0
2798	Miscellaneous	26	0
2799	**Total Fringes**		**11,663**
	Total		**128,672**

Electricians make light. The difference between Electricians and Grips in very broad terms is that Electricians make light and Grips shade it. The Electric Department is responsible for all things electric on set. They operate the generators, rig and set the lights, keep batteries recharged, and generally handle anything relating to electric power.

Traditionally, generators and batteries are handled by members of Local 40 of the International Brotherhood of Electrical Workers (IBEW) instead of the International Alliance of Theatrical Stage Employees (IATSE), but some companies work on location with only IATSE members if they have a union crew.

Electricity is very dangerous and must be handled only by those who know their tools well. Hiring inexperienced electricians is asking for accidents which could hurt or even kill people. It has happened in the past. Therefore, the choice of Electric Department personnel is very important for safety on the set.

2701   Chief Lighting Technician

Description	Amount	Units	X	Rate	Subtotal
Prep	0	Week	1	1,945.30	0
Shoot	4	Weeks	1	1,945.30	7,781
Wrap	0	Week	1	1,945.30	0
					7,781
Overtime allowance	10	%	1	0	0
Personal Equipment Rental	10	Weeks	1	0	0
Car Allowance	0	Weeks	1	0	0
Total					**7,781**

BUDBOOK.MMB 2,671,976 / Category 2700 128,672 / Account 2701 7,781 — Cume: 0 Change: 0

The Chief Lighting Technician formerly was known as the *Gaffer*. This person is the head of the Electric Department. He or she will bring in the rest of the electric crew and the UPM will do the actual hiring. This is normal for all the departments. The head of each department will bring in a list of people for that department and the UPM will approve them, or hire them. The next step in the hiring process is to make sure that each person has been trained in the use of the tools for that department. As we discussed before, the certificate of training must be kept on file in the office. Then, and only then, can the employee go to work.

A good Chief Lighting Technician will save us countless thousands of dollars and hours of grief. An extreme example is a Gaffer I knew in New York who regularly saved his Directors of Photography from embarrassment due to their inept lighting techniques. He has since become a D.P. himself, by the way.

Independent Contractor: Sometimes employees will ask to be hired as independent contractors. Unless their works falls within strict legal guidelines, this is a terrible idea. An independent contractor is not just any employee. The concept of the independent contractor was designed for, say, a house painter. We would give a house painter a week to paint the front of the house and $2,000. We would not tell the painter when to arrive and when to leave nor would we give the painter any tools. Therefore an employer can neither tell an independent contractor what hours to work nor provide the tools to be used. A crew member who appears on the call sheet or production report must be by law an employee. A person who is a member of a department which supplies the tools of the trade must be an employee.

It is always better policy for a company to work within the legal guidelines. Here's one very good reason: A company I know hired a driver as an independent contractor. When the show was over the driver absent mindedly applied for unemployment insurance, something not due independent contractors. The employee realized the mistake and tried to withdraw the application, but it was too late. The Employment Development Division of the state government investigated, and the company was fined over $30,000 for trying to avoid paying unemployment taxes.

2702 Best Boy
"Best Boy" is another generic term meaning the second in command of a particular department. So there might be a Best Boy Grip. Used by itself, it means the second electrician.

2703 Company Electricians
A "Juicer" is an electrician in old Hollywood patois. It describes the job so well that I use it even though it faded from the scene years ago.

2706 Generator Operator
More often than not the Driver of our Electric/Grip truck also will function as our Generator Operator. If not, our Gaffer or Best Boy will. A Hollywood local of the IBEW (40) for Generator Operators still operates, primarily on major studio lots where the generators are physically separated from the sound stages. In that case we must hire the studio's Generator Operator and pay overtime in the rare instance that we must film after 5:30 PM.

2707-08 Pre-Rig and Strike Crew
Here is one of those cases where we can save our company thousands of dollars by spending hundreds. If we have a large set or vast location area it generally pays to have a rigging crew prewire it before the shooting crew arrives. Remember, when the shooting crew is there we are paying Actors, Director, and other people while the Electricians run cables. This time is expensive. Hiring two or three people the day before to run cables and bring some lights onto the set will save thousands in setup time the next day. Likewise, when the set is wrapped, it will save even more money to send two or three people back the next day to wrap the cables and whatever lights are left, than to work a dead-tired crew on overtime

2709 Generator Rental
I have rented generators for activities other than filming. When we were building the sets for *War and Remembrance*, for instance, the warehouse in which we were constructing could not supply enough power to run all the machine tools. Then when the prerig crew arrived to light the set even more power was needed to rig all the lights and test them. So we rented extra generators to supply our needs.

Rentals

```
MMB  Movie Magic Budgeting - [BUDBOOK.MMB   2710 - Equipment Rentals]      _ 🗗 ✕
MMB  File  Edit  Setup  Tools  Library  Go To  Magic  Window  Help          _ 🗗 ✕
BUDBOOK.MMB          2,671,976                            TOP SHEET         Cume:      0
Category 2700          128,672                            ACCOUNT           Change:    0
Account 2710           75,000                             DETAIL
#  %  F  $
```

Description	Amount	Units	X	Rate	Subtotal	
Studio Electric Package	0	Week	1	0	0	
Location Electric Package	10	Weeks	1	7,500	75,000	
HMI Lights Rentals	0	Week	1	0	0	
HMI Lights Time Charges	0	Week	1	0	0	
Dimmers/Transformers	0	Day	1	0	0	
Arcs	0	Day	1	0	0	
Extra Night Package	0	Day	1	0	0	
Electric Box Rentals	0	Day	1	0	0	
Total					**75,000**	

Studio Electric Package

Most rental studios (and which of them is not these days?) have an arrangement which will supply us with an electric package whether we want it or not. Most of the time this is a convenience. It eliminates the need to offload our equipment when we move into the studio, reload our van when we move out, and in general can save us money over the cost of the van.

It can also be a very large pain. Consider the following case. We have contracted to rent a production van for an eight-week shoot. The price we negotiated for tractor with generators, 40-foot trailer, and an electric/grip package is based on eight solid weeks of use. Now we find that our Director cannot agree to an interior location for a key set shooting for weeks 5 and 6. We are forced to rent a studio and build the set for those two weeks of shooting. Because of the studio equipment package we must rent, we cannot use our own rented van and equipment for weeks 5 and 6, even though all our equipment is right for the shoot, and the studio has different kinds of equipment, which we will now have to make work somehow. What to do?

We can return our van to the rental facility and take it off rental for the two weeks. The rental company then can rent equipment off our van to other companies during the interim, and we will never know whether our equipment will be returned to us in the same condition in which we turned it in. We can pay the two weeks rental for the van as well as the studio equipment, plus whatever it costs to store the thing. Or we can try to buy off the company that has the equipment rental concession with the studio we are renting. Whatever we do, we must be sure that the studio rental package is spelled out clearly before we take up residence so that we can cope with such problems.

HMI Lights and Time Charges

HMI lights were introduced to the movie business to replace the large, cumbersome arc and incandescent lights. Their light is generated by a quartz bulb, much like our car headlight. They use less power, are far lighter, and are more expensive and finicky than regular lights. It is a common practice when a rental company rents us HMI lights to charge us by the hour for their use. It is possible but unlikely to make an "all-in" deal for the lights and eliminate the time charge by paying more per day of rental.

Extra Night Package

There will be times when, for a night or two or five, we will need to light up an entire exterior of a city block or more. Obviously, we do not have that much equipment on our truck, so we make a deal with our electric supplier to rent an auxiliary package just for that period of time.

Another kind of night lighting package, the *Solarc* System, can make an excellent source for moonlight, or even a soft night-style light for the entire set with a single source.

Electric Box Rental

Our Gaffer or Best Boy will have a large box filled with gels and other light-modifying substances to rent to us, usually at far less than our electric supplier (see expendables later).

2711 Musco Lights

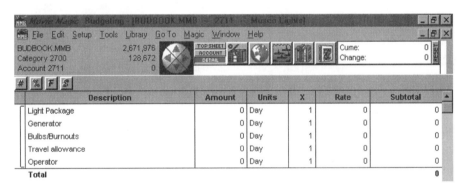

Musco Lights can cast a tremendous amount of light over a very wide area. They consist of 16 12k HMI lights, individually aimed, on a platform atop an extended arm that can be maneuvered to aim in any direction. Two Musco lights were used to light up the entire Statue of Liberty in its Centennial celebration, for instance. Expensive, but well worth it if we have to light up a whole football field at night or a battleground.

2713 Purchases
Burnouts

Sometimes we can make a deal with our equipment provider which will enable us to cover this cost in the rental of the lights.

Expendables

Expendables are those items, excluding bulbs, which are used up in the course of a production, like rolls of gel, battens, or magic markers.

2800   Grip Operations

Acct#	Account Title	Page	Total
2801	Key Grip	27	7,781
2802	Second Grip	27	7,034
2803	Dolly Grip	27	7,034
2804	Crane Grip	27	0
2805	Crane Driver	27	0
2806	Company Grips	27	13,440
2807	Extra Grips	27	13,440
2808	Local Hires	27	0
2809	Rigging Crew	27	0
2810	Striking Crew	27	0
2811	Tent/Shelter Erection	28	0
2812	Grip Package	28	40,000
2813	Special Equipment	28	0
2814	Dolly Rental	28	0
2815	Equipment Purchase	28	0
2816	Crane	28	0
2897	Loss & Damage	28	0
2898	Miscellaneous	28	0
2899	**Total Fringes**		**14,537**
	Total		**103,266**

BUDBOOK.MMB   2,671,976   Category 2800   103,266   Cume: 0   Change: 0

Moxie Magic Budgeting - [BUDBOOK.MMB - 2800 - Grip Operations]
File   Edit   Setup   Tools   Library   Go To   Magic   Window   Help

If Electricians make light, grips shade it. They have many interesting instruments with which to do this, everything from *Targets* which are opaque, black circular pieces of fabric in frames) to *Flags* (rectangular pieces of fabric in the same mode) to *Cucaloris* or "Cookies" (patterned flags designed to give mottled shading). These are usually held up on *C-stands*, which in turn are counterbalanced by *Sandbags*, which weigh down the legs to keep the whole thing upright. If something is not high enough, including some actors, grips can provide *Apple Boxes*, sturdy wooden boxes that can easily carry the weight of a man, to raise the object, or if not so much height is needed, *Half-apples* will be used. If just one leg of a chair must be raised, wooden *Risers* can be used, or even Wedges. These are only a few of the many Grips' tools.

In a great sense, the Electric and Grip departments are twins. Normally the Chief Lighting Technician and Key Grip will make the same salary, work the same prep and wrap times, and so forth. The second in command in each department will do the same, and the company electricians and company grips will do the same. Differences arise with equipment rental and the kinds of equipment used.

2801 Key Grip

| | File | Edit | Setup | Tools | Library | Go To | Magic | Window | Help | | | | |

	Description	Amount	Units	X	Rate	Subtotal	
•	Prep	0	Week	1	1,945.30	0	
•	Shoot	4	Weeks	1	1,945.30	7,781	
•	Wrap	0	Week	1	1,945.30	0	
						7,781	
	Overtime allowance	10	%	1	0	0	
•	Personal Equipment Rental	10	Weeks	1	0	0	
	Car Allowance	0	Weeks	1	0	0	
	Total					**7,781**	

The Key Grip needs time to prepare a show. Prior to filming, locations must be seen, equipment ordered and loaded in an easily manageable manner onto the trucks, and so forth.

Grips do all sorts of things in addition to shading the lights, such as moving dollies around and putting up tents.

2802 Second Grip

Why isn't this person called the *Best Boy Grip*? I don't know. Sometimes he or she is.

Second Grip usually spends some time prepping with the Key grip and of course, is there after filming to help return the grip equipment to the rental house.

2803 Dolly Grip

This is a very specialized craft. The Dolly Grip usually works neither prep nor wrap, but has the sole responsibility of tending to the dolly. It looks like fun, but the work actually is very demanding. The Dolly Grip has practiced this craft to the point where dollying smoothly is second nature.

The Dolly Grip must be familiar with all the dollies we will be using, from doorway dollies to western dollies, Elemacks to Hustlers. And he or she must know how to recharge the hydraulics and how to manage smooth boom shots without jerking the camera at the beginning and end of the shot. When a dolly shot is planned, the dolly grip is in charge of leveling the dolly, using small wedges under the tracks until they are absolutely level so that the dolly will track without tilting the camera.

2804-05 Crane Grip and Driver

Cranes, especially the large ones, deserve a great deal of respect. The drivers and grips who operate them must be experts in many things to work them properly. Imagine trying to perform a dolly shot with a three-ton truck while the camera is mounted on a 25-foot high boom. The driver and grip have to work in absolute lockstep so that the moves are what the Director intended.

Then there is the little matter of balance. A camera, crew, and Director have to be balanced by heavy weights at the opposite end of the boom so that the Crane Grip can raise or lower the boom arm by a touch of the hand. This requires very careful adjustment of the metal weights and the mercury reservoirs inside the boom to provide that delicate balance necessary to boom smoothly. And, after the shot when the camera platform is lowered to the ground, before the crew can step off the platform they must wait until the Crane Grip has rebalanced the arm so that it won't suddenly shoot upwards and catapult the Director over the heads of the cast. The counterweights have to be re-figured to allow the camera platform end to have the heaviest weight.

2806 Company Grips

Company Grips do most of the *shading* of the light. They set the flags and stands in front of the big lights set up by the electricians. One or two usually are around for prep and wrap, because some of the equipment will be quite heavy and require three people to maneuvre it into and out of the trucks.

2807 Extra Grips

By the same thought behind hiring extra Electricians for night filming, we also need extra Grips.

2809-10 Rigging and Striking Crew

Like the Electric rigging crew, the Grip rigging crew goes into a location ahead of the shooting crew; for instance, to hang black velour or plastic outside the windows to turn daytime interiors into night shots.

2811   Equipment Rental
Grip Package

The grip package usually is rented at the same time and from the same place as the electrical package, and the whole is rented along with the production van and generators. Sometimes we will split the rentals between two or three suppliers, and that option always should be left open because it may save us money.

2813 Special Equipment

Description	Amount	Units	X	Rate	Subtotal	
Car Mounts	0		1	0	0	
Special Lift Mounts	0		1	0	0	
(e.g. Condor)	0		1	0	0	
Remote Mounts	0		1	0	0	
Total					**0**	

Car Mounts

Car mounts are usually rented from one of our own grip employees who has made them for just this purpose. Sometimes we have to mount our camera outside the driver's side window, or the passenger window, or both, to photograph the occupants of a car in motion. Car mounts, as indicated here, look like the tray you get at a drive-in restaurant, from which you eat your food. However, the car mounts are very heavy-duty, having to withstand the jouncing of the car in motion. We also can use the mounts to put lights outside the window for night shots.

2814 Dolly Rental

Description	Amount	Units	X	Rate	Subtotal	
Western Dolly	0		1	0	0	
Doorway Dolly	0		1	0	0	
Peewee	0		1	0	0	
Hustler	0		1	0	0	
Elemack	0		1	0	0	
Dolly Track	0	Foot	1	0	0	
Risers	0		1	0	0	
Jib Arms	0		1	0	0	
Outriggers	0		1	0	0	
Remote Control Dollies	0		1	0	0	
Computer Control Systems	0		1	0	0	
Total					**0**	

We almost always rent dollies from Fisher or Chapman or both. At times the grip package supplier may rent them and make them part of that package. The cost usually is the same in either case. A very important thing to remember is that there never seems to be enough dollies to go around, so as soon as we know what kind we want we should immediately call the supplier and reserve one.

Tyler System

I put this in the grip budget because it usually falls to the grips to install the device in the helicopter, anyway. The Tyler Mount was invented back in the mid-1960's by Nelson Tyler, a brilliant camera operator and tinkerer. It almost completely isolates the camera from the vibrations of a helicopter.

2815 Equipment Purchase

Description	Amount	Units	X	Rate	Subtotal
Window Gel	0		1	0	0
Scrim Material	0		1	0	0
Battens	0		1	0	0
Total					**0**

As we can see, there are a few items which will be purchased for the use of the Grip department. These are usually purchased in rolls of gel or bundles of battens, etc. And not to forget that we will have to dispose of the unused gel properly. These things can no longer just be thrown out.

2816 Crane

Description	Amount	Units	X	Rate	Subtotal
Tulip	1		1	0	0
Shotmaker	1		1	0	0
Louma	1		1	0	0
Apollo	1		1	0	0
Nike	1		1	0	0
Titan	1		1	0	0
Houston Fearless	1		1	0	0
Total					**0**

Movie Magic Budgeting - [BUDBOOK.MMB - 2816 - Crane]
File Edit Setup Tools Library Go To Magic Window Help
BUDBOOK.MMB   2,671,976   Cume: 0
Category 2800   103,266   Change: 0
Account 2816   0

As we can see, cranes come in many sizes and shapes. Our grip department will help us to choose the one which fills our picture's needs. And always remember to hire crane operators and drivers who are expert in that kind of crane.

2900 Production Sound

The original movie syntax was a silent one. Indeed, Charlie Chaplin still was making silent films years after *The Jazz Singer* opened. There was a very interesting and satisfying comfort to watching a silent film. It also was far less expensive to produce. The entire sound part of the budget was unnecessary. And different versions did not have to be made for different countries in different languages. Only the title cards had to be changed.

The sound film has long since reached its maturity, and those who feel that we "lost" something when sound took over are begging the issue. Sound film has by now progressed far beyond the state of the silents at their best, no doubt about it. The sound mixer and the post-production sound people add just as much to the artistic quality of a film as anyone else.

Movie Magic Budgeting - [BUDBOOK.MMB - 2900 - Production Sound]

File Edit Setup Tools Library Go To Magic Window Help

BUDBOOK.MMB   2,671,976   TOP SHEET   Cume: 0
Category 2900   43,328   ACCOUNT   Change: 0
                                      DETAIL

Acct#	Account Title	Page	Total
2901	Production Mixer	29	12,522
2902	Boom Operator	29	8,448
2903	Cable Puller	29	0
2904	Utility Man	29	0
2905	Playback	29	0
2906	P.A.	29	0
2907	Sound Equipment	30	15,000
2908	Set Communications	30	1,250
2909	Special Equipment Rentals	30	0
2910	Purchases	30	0
2997	Loss & Damage	30	0
2998	Miscellaneous	30	0
2999	**Total Fringes**		**6,108**
	Total		**43,328**

2901 Production Sound Mixer

Movie Magic Budgeting - [BUDBOOK.MMB - 2901 - Production Mixer]

File Edit Setup Tools Library Go To Magic Window Help

BUDBOOK.MMB   2,672,212   TOP SHEET   Cume: 0
Category 2900   43,328   ACCOUNT   Change: 0
Account 2901   12,522   DETAIL

Description	Amount	Units	X	Rate	Subtotal
Prep	0	Week	1	3,130.40	0
Shoot	4	Weeks	1	3,130.40	12,522
Wrap	0	Week	1	3,130.40	0
					12,522
Overtime allowance	10	%	1	0	0
Personal Equipment Rental	10	Weeks	1	0	0
Car Allowance	0	Week	1	0	0
Total					**12,522**

This is definitely one area in which cost must not be an issue. A good Mixer can save us thousands of dollars in ADR fees in post-production.

Furthermore it always is a good idea to rent the mixer's own sound equipment. He or she may have built it personally, or at least modified it to specific standards, and it is far more reliable than rented equipment because it is maintained personally by the Mixer on a daily basis.

ADR: Automatic Dialogue Replacement, or looping, which is what the Actor will have to do in post-production to atone for the sins of the mixer.

2902 Boom Operator

Boom Operators handle the microphone boom, that long fishing-pole looking device that sticks into the set with the mike at the end of it, pointing toward the actors. A good Boom Operator can save us immense amounts of money in post-production sound correction. At times, a Cable Puller or Utility Person, or even another member of the crew, will have to work a second boom to get proper sound for a particular scene. Or we may need another pair of hands to handle the wireless microphone receivers.

2903 Cable Puller

If we have no Cable Puller nobody will be pulling the cable behind the Boom Operator while tracking backwards with dolly shots. And if nobody pulls the cable, members of the crew will trip over it (see Insurance).

2905 Playback

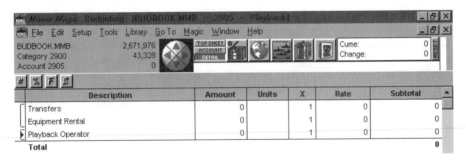

Playback occurs when we have an Actor who sings or a band that plays on camera. Usually we have prerecorded both the band and the singer, and the singer is singing along with the recording while the cameras are rolling. The recording is played back by the Playback people. It is not normal to record sound while playback is being played, but there will be times when we will start playback to get a roomful of people dancing in time to the music, cut the playback to record the sound, and the people will keep dancing to the music that they can no longer hear. Likewise, the band keeps miming the act of playing their instruments. For inexperienced extras, this usually causes hilarity far beyond its stimulus.

2906   Public Address System (P.A.)

If we have large numbers of extras or are filming in an area of exceptionally loud ambient sound, this might be necessary.

2907   Sound Equipment

We will try to rent our equipment from our mixer, who also maintains it.

2908   Communications
Walkie-Talkies

When I first started working in this business there were no walkie-talkies for the movie industry. We ran and we yelled. We used signal flags, mirrors, lights, anything that worked. Walkie-talkies were strange things used by the Army in World War II. Today, A.D.s are stressed if they are not supplied with walkie-talkies with microphone extensions or headsets. I suppose that's progress.

When we budget for walkie-talkies we must be sure to include plenty. Walkie-talkies suddenly, unexpectedly will run down their batteries. So we must also rent the rechargers and recharge the batteries every night. Furthermore, it is wise to rent walkie-talkies that have several channels, as the lighting crew will want to have its own, as well as the drivers, and production – you get the picture.

Good practice would be to have each crew member who needs one sign out a walkie-talkie every morning and sign it in at night, with someone like the DGA trainee keeping track of the serial numbers. If that is done, we will know immediately if someone has lost or "borrowed" a walkie-talkie. They now can cost over $2,000 each, so it is a good idea to keep close track of them during shooting.

Beepers

Beepers can be very handy things when we are wondering why the set isn't ready for us to film and the Art Director has vanished.

Portable Phones

Portable phones have become ubiquitous in all walks of life. Grips and Electricians use them on the set to order equipment. Drivers order trucks. Directors order lunch. Just be careful about using them too much as the air-time costs can mount alarmingly.

Another caution: I have made it a practice never to talk on the phone while I am driving a moving vehicle. As a passenger, yes, but not as a driver. Several European countries have already made it illegal to talk on the phone while driving, and with luck the United States will follow suit soon.

3000 Mechanical Effects

Acct#	Account Title	Page	Total
3001	Key Man	30	7,848
3002	Assistant	30	0
3003	Extra Help	31	0
3004	Local Hires	31	0
3005	Rigging Crew	31	0
3006	Striking Crew	31	0
3007	Manufacturing	31	0
3008	Equipment Rental	31	0
3009	Material rental	31	0
3010	Purchases	31	0
3011	Shop Rental	31	0
3012	Firearms/Weapons	31	0
3013	Electronic Effects	32	0
3014	Explosions	32	0
3015	Permits	32	0
3016	Weather	32	0
3017	Office Expenses	32	0
3018	FX Package	32	0
3097	Loss & Damage	32	0
3098	Miscellaneous	32	0

Mechanical Effects occur in real time in front of the camera: gunshots, explosions, broken windows, people breaking furniture over each other's heads. Anything that actually happens in front of the camera.

As with stunts, safety is the overwhelmingly important factor here. If we don't know the special effects people we must check with the UPMs of their last two or three shows to see how well they did, whether they followed all the safety requirements, and so on.

3001 Keyman

Description	Amount	Units	X	Rate	Subtotal
Prep	0	Week	1	1,962.10	0
Shoot	4	Weeks	1	1,962.10	7,848
Wrap	0	Week	1	1,962.10	0
					7,848
Overtime allowance	10	%	1	0	0
Personal Equipment Rental	10	Weeks	1	0	0
Car Allowance	0	Week	1	0	0
Total					7,848

The Special Effects Keyman is one of the most important people on our crew, in charge of our Special Effects Department. Many keymen travel with a complete mobile machine shop and can fabricate things on short notice, or repair things that are obscure to the lay person. Whenever a special effect is called for, it is absolutely essential that the keyman be included on the location scout to see where the effect will happen, that he (or she) be given adequate preparation time. The special effects keyman needs enough time to prepare the show prior to filming so that each effect can be performed with maximum safety in mind. Don't for a moment assume that we know more about safety than this person. We do not.

When effects and stunts are combined it also is essential that the effects person and stunt gaffer work out their problems together. Safety demands this.

At all times, safety should be uppermost in our mind. No matter what the pressure of budget or schedules, no movie or TV show is worth an injury of any kind. Take the time to allow the effects and stunt people proper prep, and they will ensure the well-being of the cast and crew.

3002 Assistant
Sometimes a single effects person is not enough. Extra effects people must be called in to help whenever necessary.

3005-06 Rig and Strike Crews
Once again, a prerig of an elaborate effect will save valuable crew time.

3008 Special Effects Equipment

Fire Prevention
We will need to keep on the set, close at hand, fire extinguishers that are fully charged and ready for action.

Ritters

A Ritter is a large fan, the size of an airplane propeller, encased in a safety cage, that can create a violent wind storm. Before firing up a Ritter, it is essential to be sure that nothing can blow around that is not intended to do so.

Rain Birds

Rain Birds are very tall sprinklers that emulate a rain storm. They usually are used when the scene calls for rain; the weather bureau has predicted rain, so naturally it is clear as a bell. Rain Birds are very impartial about soaking crew and staff as well as actors and sets. It is wise to provide the crew and staff with water protective materials, and it is especially important to keep all the equipment dry. Electric bulbs explode when they have heated up and are suddenly soaked.

Snow Throwers

I find that when I have to fill a street with snow and it hasn't snowed recently, I can call the local airport and ask for their foam maker, if they can spare it for a few minutes. The foam substance used to blanket runways for emergency landings looks exactly like snow on the ground, can be laid over a large area in a surprisingly short time, and biodegrades nicely shortly thereafter.

Foggers

I really hate foggers. Right after *Blade Runner* every two-bit movie and TV show had to have the sets filled with fog in order to be artistic. Fog should be used sparingly and only when it achieves some purpose. Even then, the crew must be warned that fog will be used, and supplied with face masks. We don't know who on the crew is asthmatic.

3010 Purchases

Description	Amount	Units	X	Rate	Subtotal
Fire Extinguishers	0		1	0	0
Expendables	0		1	0	0
Bullet Hits	0		1	0	0
Squibs	0		1	0	0
Breakaways	0		1	0	0
Pyrotechnics	0		1	0	0
Total					**0**

Obviously it will be up to the Effects Keyman to obtain all the preceding devices.

Squibs: Those tiny bags filled with gunpowder that emulate bullet hits on the human body. Usually they are accompanied by tiny bags of blood so the "spurt" can be seen by the camera. The Actor always must be protected by a hard shield, usually of metal, between the body and the squib

Breakaways: Manufactured from very light materials such as balsa wood. That's the furniture part, anyway. Breakaway glass now is made of very light plastic that appears to shatter much as real glass does, but actually is easily broken and has no sharp edges. We call it *candy glass* because in the early days it was made of spun sugar. Sometimes, in the background of a shot in an early movie, you can see a hungry extra taking a bite out of a broken window.

3013 Electronics Effects

	Description	Amount	Units	X	Rate	Subtotal	
	Computer Design	0		1	0	0	
	Video Transfers	0		1	0	0	
	Operators	0		1	0	0	
	On-Set Equipment	0		1	0	0	
	Total					**0**	

Music Magic Budgeting - [BUDBOOK.MMB — 3013 — Electronic Effects]
File Edit Setup Tools Library Go To Magic Window Help
BUDBOOK.MMB   2,671,976   Cume: 0
Category 3000   10,379   Change: 0
Account 3013   0

Some years ago I did a picture called *Futureworld* in which we had large banks of computer screens, each with a different sort of readout on it. It all looked very futuristic and very efficient. Most of it was gibberish, of course. But someone had to program the computers to show all that balderdash on the screens, and that person took some weeks to work out the problems, not the least of which was to have the proper things show up on the proper screens on cue.

3018 Effects Package

Most Effects Keymen travel with a mobile effects shop. For shows heavy in effects, I have made a package deal with Effects people, an all-in price agreed on before filming, including personnel and materials. All this must be spelled out very carefully prior to filming, so that if the Director changes changes the specs for an effect, the proper adjustment can be made in the agreed on price.

3100 Special Visual Effects

Acct#	Account Title	Page	Total
3101	Rear Projection	32	0
3102	Front Projection	32	0
3103	Holography	32	0
3104	Optical Effects	32	0
3105	Mattes	32	0
3106	Glass Shots	33	0
3107	Blue Screen	33	0
3108	Rotoscope Photography	33	0
3109	FX Shop	33	0
3110	Introvision	33	0
3111	Miniatures	33	0
3112	Computer Generated FX	33	0
3113	Office Expenses	33	0
3197	Loss & Damage	33	0
3198	Miscellaneous	33	0
3199	**Total Fringes**		**0**
	Total		**0**

The art of visual effects progresses almost daily. A few excellent companies create for the screen whatever we can imagine. Glance over the list of possibilities above and you'll see some of the options available.

The best procedure for estimating something of this complexity is to submit the script to two or three of these companies and allow them to make a proposal. We will be able to see how each plans to approach our visual problem and what steps – and at what cost – can we arrive at a good conclusion.

3109 FX Shop

For many years when the major studios ruled the movie business each studio had its own captive office of wizards whose purpose was to amaze and delight the audience with their visual legerdemain. People like L. B. Abbott at Fox and the amazing Ray Harryhausen worked for years producing astounding effects that could be accomplished only on the screen.

Today as Independent Producers take over a larger and larger portion of the distribution pie, independent special effects shops have grown up in Hollywood. Dreamquest is one of the better ones, as is Industrial Light and Magic, which caters to Lucasfilm and Steven Spielberg's Amblin' Entertainment. These shops are able to mix visual, electronic, digital, and editorial effects so that anything conceivable can be realized on screen. As Dr. Edwin Land, inventor of the Polaroid camera once said, "What the mind can conceive, man can achieve."

3110 Introvision

I include Introvision as a separate item because it seems to provide a unique service. Tom Naud of Introvision showed me a demo of the firm's system in which Adolf Hitler walked into a conference room, around the conference table, and out a side door to the room. The room existed only as a still photograph and the Actor playing old Adolf in fact was walking around on a limbo set. But it was all done in real time, and when Adolf rested his hands on the table, I would have sworn that it was all real. Obviously, it was far less expensive to use Introvision to re-create the conference room than it would have been to reconstruct the room itself.

3200   Set Operations

Acct#	Account Title	Page	Total
3201	Set Carpenter	33	6,418
3202	Standby Painter	33	8,557
3203	Greens Department	34	6,723
3204	Craft Service	34	21,415
3205	First Aid	34	5,637
3206	Set Security	34	0
3207	Set Firemen	34	0
3208	Office Expenses	34	0
3209	Weather Service	34	0
3210	Portable Bathrooms	35	0
3211	Courtesy Payments	35	0
3297	Loss & Damage	35	0
3298	Miscellaneous	35	0
3299	**Total Fringes**		**11,401**
	Total		**60,151**

Set Operations cover all kinds of functions that do not fit properly into any other category. Several members of the shooting crew work alone on the set without having a department, and here is where we budget for them. Some budgets include Grips in this department, but the Grip Department has enough personnel and enough specialized equipment to be a department on its own.

3201   Set Carpenter

Description	Amount	Units	X	Rate	Subtotal
Prep	0	Week	1	1,604.40	0
Shoot	4	Weeks	1	1,604.40	6,418
Wrap	0	Week	1	1,604.40	0
					6,418
Personal Equipment Rental	10	Weeks	1	0	0
Lumber Purchases	0		1	0	0
Tool Purchases	0		1	0	0
Misc. Equipment Purchases	0		1	0	0
Car Allowance	0	Week	1	0	0
Total					**6,418**

The Set Carpenter needs neither prep nor wrap time, but is there only during the shoot to help out with wood problems. A Set Carpenter can cover a multitude of sins, especially if the dolly grip bangs the dolly into the

wall of the 200-year-old mansion we are using as a location. A Set
Carpenter also is known as a Prop Maker in union terms.

3202   Set Painter

Movie Magic Budgeting - [BUDBOOK.MMB – 3202 – Standby Painter]					
File Edit Setup Tools Library Go To Magic Window Help					
BUDBOOK.MMB 2,671,976 Category 3200 60,151 Account 3202 8,557				Cume: 0 Change: 0	
Description	**Amount**	**Units**	**X**	**Rate**	**Subtotal**
Prep	0	Week	1	2,139.20	0
Shoot	4	Weeks	1	2,139.20	8,557
Wrap	0	Week	1	2,139.20	0
					8,557
Overtime allowance	10	%	1	0	0
Personal Equipment Rental	10	Weeks	1	0	0
Paint Purchases	0		1	0	0
Brush Purchases	0		1	0	0
Misc. Equipment Purchases	0		1	0	0
Car Allowance	0	Week	1	0	0
Total					**8,557**

Set Painters stay on the set during filming to supply whatever paint
exigencies may arise. Usually these are qualified as Sign Painters who can
whip up a respectable shop sign in a trice.

3203   Greens Department

Movie Magic Budgeting - [BUDBOOK.MMB – 3203 – Greens Department]					
File Edit Setup Tools Library Go To Magic Window Help					
BUDBOOK.MMB 2,671,976 Category 3200 60,151 Account 3203 6,723				Cume: 0 Change: 0	
Description	**Amount**	**Units**	**X**	**Rate**	**Subtotal**
Prep	0	Week	1	1,680.70	0
Shoot	4	Weeks	1	1,680.70	6,723
Wrap	0	Week	1	1,680.70	0
					6,723
Overtime allowance	10	%	1	0	0
Personal Equipment Rental	10	Weeks	1	0	0
Car Allowance	0	Week	1	0	0
Greens Purchased	0		1	0	0
Greens Rented	0		1	0	0
Greensman Box Rental	0		1	0	0
Total					**6,723**

Greens are exactly that – plants, trees, shrubs, cacti, anything living that
has an appendage planted in the ground. Greens people will do wonderful
things to mask the terrible things other people do. I just did a show that
took place in Connecticut. The neighborhood we filmed in Los Angeles to
emulate Connecticut had some very un-Hartford-like palm trees. Our greens
folk covered the bases of the palms with East Coast shrubs.

On the other hand, when filming *Hello Dolly!* in Upstate New York we rebuilt an entire town (Garrison) to look like Yonkers, NY, at the turn of the century. What did we do with the commuters who rode the train to New York every day to work from Garrison? Where did they park their cars? We built a huge 1900-style barn to cover the cars.

Of course there always is one malcontent, and this one didn't use the barn. He always parked his car right next to our vintage railroad station, an anachronism beyond belief. He had just as much right to be there as we did. So every day we covered his car with shrubs and bushes to disguise it, and before he returned home we uncovered the car and cleaned it off so that he would not know. One day he came home early and found his car covered with shrubs. From that day forth he parked his car in a different spot each day near the station. So if we see the movie today we might notice a large shrub that appears to jump randomly around the area next to the railroad station.

3204 Craft Service

Description	Amount	Units	X	Rate	Subtotal	
Prep	0	Week	1	1,603.70	0	
Shoot	4	Weeks	1	1,603.70	6,415	
Wrap	0	Week	1	1,603.70	0	
					6,415	
Overtime allowance	10	%	1	0	0	
Personal Equipment Rental	10	Weeks	1	250	2,500	
Supplies Purchased	10	Weeks	1	1,250	12,500	
Set Coffee/Water/Ice	10	Weeks	1	0	0	
Set Munchies	10	Weeks	1	0	0	
Car Allowance	0	Week	1	0	0	
Total					**21,415**	

This person keeps the coffee hot, sweeps the floor when we spill stuff, and generally does everything that nobody else wants to do. Craft Service also keeps a table of goodies for the crew to nibble on during the shoot. These usually include coffee and donuts or sticky buns in the morning, cookies in the afternoon. There also is always a bottle of aspirin and a cooler with soft drinks handy, and the inevitable water cooler.

Recently a couple of good companies have arisen that purvey craft service to movies. Because they supply several shows simultaneously they can afford to purchase their supplies in bulk and pass the savings on to us.

3205   First Aid

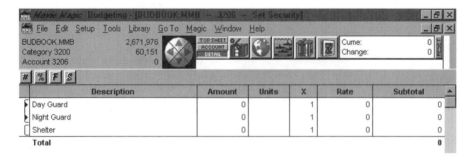

	Description	Amount	Units	X	Rate	Subtotal	
•	Prep	0	Week	1	1,409.170	0	
•	Shoot	4	Weeks	1	1,409.170	5,637	
•	Wrap	0	Week	1	1,409.170	0	
						5,637	
	Overtime allowance	10	%	1	0	0	
	Personal Equipment Rental	0	Week	1	0	0	
	Car Allowance	0	Week	1	0	0	
•	Supplies	10	Weeks	1	0	0	
	Standby Ambulance	0		1	0	0	
	Standby Paramedics	0		1	0	0	
	Total					**5,637**	

No law states that we must have a First Aid person on set at all times, although some of the unions have it in their contracts. No other business in the world has such a requirement. On the other hand, if a lamp falls on a member of the crew, OSHA will always investigate. If it is discovered that we did not have a medic standing by we can be fined quite heavily for not looking after the welfare of the crew. And if the same lamp falls on an actor, it could cost a great deal more than the cost of the First Aid person. Of course if the lamp falls on the First Aid person . . .

3206   Set Security

	Description	Amount	Units	X	Rate	Subtotal	
	Day Guard	0		1	0	0	
	Night Guard	0		1	0	0	
	Shelter	0		1	0	0	
	Total					**0**	

Once we have spent $50,000 to build a set, we may wish to have it guarded over the weekend so that the locals don't make off with our set dressing.

3300 Wardrobe Department

Acct#	Account Title	Page	Total
3301	Costume Designer	35	0
3302	Assistant Designer	35	0
3303	Men's Costumer	35	6,376
3304	Assistant Men's Costumer	35	5,547
3305	Extra Men's Costumers	36	0
3306	Local Hires	36	0
3307	Ladies' Costumers	36	6,376
3308	Asst. Ladies' Costumer	36	5,547
3309	Extra Ladies' Costumers	36	0
3310	Local Hires	36	0
3311	Seamstresses	37	0
3312	Manufacture	37	0
3313	Rentals	37	0
3314	Purchases	37	0
3315	Alterations	37	0
3316	Cleaning	37	0
3317	Office	37	0
3397	Loss & Damage	37	0
3398	Miscellaneous	37	0
3399	**Total Fringes**		**8,384**

The most important aspect of wardrobe is that it must be appropriate. It must be part of the whole picture. It cannot stand out. The genius of an Edith Head or a Theoni V. Aldredge is that their wardrobe designs perfectly complemented everything else about the films for which they designed.

3301 Costume Designer

Description	Amount	Units	X	Rate	Subtotal
Prep	0	Week	1	4,000	0
Shoot	0	Weeks	1	4,000	0
					0
Personal Equipment Rental	0	Weeks	1	0	0
Car Allowance	0	Week	1	0	0
Total					**0**

Much of the time we won't need a Costume Designer *per se*. Only in period pieces or highly stylized films, including Sci-Fi films, are Costume Designers really necessary. It is important that the wardrobe of a film have a consistent feel to it. Sometimes a good shopper can do that for you.

Many times the actors will be able to wear their own clothes for contemporary pieces. For those times that we are dealing with clothes that cannot be off the rack, though, a designer is very necessary.

Designers need much prep and no wrap. Other members of the department need wrap time to return the clothing to the rental houses, but the designer does not do that.

3302 Men's Costumer

At times I have hired a Men's Costumer as the head of the department. It then becomes his responsibility to hire the other wardrobe persons, arrange for the rental or purchase of wardrobe, fittings, and so forth, generally coordinating the entire department. I have also worked on shows with a primarily female cast, in which case I assigned the women's customer as head of the department.

In either case the Men's and Women's Costumers both need a considerable amount of prep time. Immediately after an Actor is signed to play a role in the picture, he or she will be sent to the costume department for measurements. Actors' composites rarely show the right measurements. And, prior to that, the Costumer and the Director must meet to discuss the style of the costumes. So quite a bit of prep time is necessary. When shooting is finished, the Costumer must return the clothing to the rental houses, so a few days of wrap is necessary.

In some cases, when the wardrobe is purchased rather than rented, the actors are given the option of buying the clothing, usually at half-price.

3307 Women's Costumer
If the cast of a show consists primarily of women, the head of the department might be the Women's Costumer.

3303, 3308 Assistant Costumers
Trying to save money by hiring too few Costumers for the amount of cast we have in the show is a really bad idea. It is important to have enough Costumers and makeup people to have the cast ready for the shot when the

camera is ready. Too few means that the whole crew, on overtime rates, will be waiting for the cast to be wardrobed. So if we have more than three or four Actors in the cast on any one day, we need to hire extra Costumers to keep everyone ready on time.

3311 Seamstresses

When first purchased, costumes will have to be fitted to the Actors. If they do not fit per the Director's instructions, they must be altered. And we can't forget that sometimes the Director wants the clothes to be ill-fitting for certain characters. So Seamstresses usually work only during the prep period of a film and occasionally during the shoot for a day or two.

3312 Manufacture

Description	Amount	Units	X	Rate	Subtotal
Men's Labor	0		1	0	0
Men's Materials	0		1	0	0
Ladies' Labor	0		1	0	0
Ladies' Materials	0		1	0	0
Extras Labor	0		1	0	0
Extras Materials	0		1	0	0
Total					**0**

Care must be taken with this department. Normally one would assume that an Actor can be easily fitted with clothes from his or her own closet or off the rack in a store. But once in a while we will be called on to cast an outsized person and this account will be necessary. I once did a TV series with an Actor who was 6' 8" tall, and every last piece of wardrobe for him had to be handmade. There weren't even racks that large!

3316 Cleaning

This is one account not to forget. Every major production center in the United States has at least one cleaner that stays open all night to handle the film traffic. And in those cities that do not, we can always pay a cleaner to stay open. Every night it will be necessary to have the wardrobe cleaned. During filming the clothes have become clogged with makeup and sweat.

This price can vary depending on the numbers of extras and principals on the set in any one day. It also can be awfully pesky, as it was on one show I did in which the producers forgot to budget for it, an oversight amounting to hundreds of dollars per week.

3398   Other Charges

Description	Amount	Units	X	Rate	Subtotal	
Storeroom Supplies	0		1	0	0	
Equipment	0		1	0	0	
Costumers' Box Rental	0		1	0	0	
Wardrobe Space Rental	0		1	0	0	
Polaroid Camera	0		1	0	0	
Polaroid Film	0		1	0	0	
Hazard/Flight/Underwater	0		1	0	0	
Shipping/Delivery	0		1	0	0	
Permits	0		1	0	0	
Total					0	

Window elements: Movie Magic Budgeting - [BUDBOOK.MMB -- 3398 -- Miscellaneous]. File Edit Setup Tools Library Go To Magic Window Help. BUDBOOK.MMB 2,671,976; Category 3300 32,230; Account 3398 0. TOP SHEET / ACCOUNT / DETAIL. Cume: 0; Change: 0.

Costumer's Box Rental

I have rented everything from just a sewing machine to an entire wardrobe department in a trailer, including washing machines, racks, ironing boards, and dressing rooms. When renting something from the head of the Wardrobe Department, check it out thoroughly to make sure that everything works, and then check with the Transportation Department to see what they can offer of the same ilk and at what price. Usually, we save money by using our employee's equipment instead of renting from the outside.

Wardrobe Department Space

If we are not operating on a major studio lot and our office space will not suffice for wardrobe fitting and storage, we must rent more space somewhere else. Most cinema wardrobe suppliers will rent us space, or perhaps a corner of a warehouse somewhere. On *War and Remembrance* we built a whole separate wardrobe department into the warehouse in which we had built the sets.

Polaroid Camera/Film

This is one department that will need Polaroid supplies. After finishing each scene the Wardrobe people will take Polaroids of all the actors for that scene, so that if retakes are necessary the wardrobe can be matched exactly. The Makeup Department likewise uses polaroids for the same purpose.

3400 Makeup and Hair Department

Acct#	Account Title	Page	Total
3401	Head Makeup Artist	38	8,786
3402	Assistant Makeup Artist	38	8,389
3403	Extra Makeup Artists	38	0
3404	Local Hires	38	0
3405	Body Makeup Artists	39	0
3406	Head Hair Stylist	39	8,786
3407	Assistant Hair Stylist	39	8,389
3408	Extra Hair Stylists	39	0
3409	Local Hires	39	0
3410	Makeup Supplies	39	0
3411	Hair Supplies	39	0
3412	Wigs/Hairpieces	39	0
3413	Special Makeup Design	39	0
3414	Prosthetics	40	0
3415	Special Appliances	40	0
3416	Rentals	40	0
3497	Loss & Damage	40	0
3498	Miscellaneous	40	0
3499	**Total Fringes**		**10,710**
	Total		**45,060**

It always is a good idea to check with the production departments of prior shows that employed the Actors we have hired to determine how long each requires in makeup every morning. Most men and children, unless there are special circumstances such as prostheses, need only 15 minutes to a half hour. On the other hand, most women require anywhere from a half-hour to (I'll never forget this one) four hours, just for a straight everyday makeup. Also, check on the Makeup Department's requirements. This will determine the call times for our Makeup Department and talent. After the first day's shooting, change the call sheet to what it should have been.

3401 Makeup Artists

Description	Amount	Units	X	Rate	Subtotal
Prep	0	Week	1	2,196.60	0
Shoot	4	Weeks	1	2,196.60	8,786
Wrap	0	Week	1	2,196.60	0
					8,786
Overtime allowance	10	%	1	0	0
Personal Equipment Rental	10	Weeks	1	0	0
Car Allowance	0	Week	1	0	0
Total					**8,786**

The Fine Art of Makeup is the ability to not only make an Actor's face acceptable for the screen but also enhance it in whatever other way is called for by the script.   This can be beauty, horror, or weather-beaten, or everything in between. Next time you get up in the morning, before you go to work, look closely at your face in the mirror. If you just glance at it, as is done 99 percent of the time, it looks like a regular face, right? Now look very closely. Even if you use makeup, there are still blemishes and patches of slightly different colors on your skin. Everyone has them. In normal everyday commerce we ignore these things. Our mind's eye adjusts, and people look pretty darned good, actually. Now look very closely at your face and imagine what it would look like if it were blown up to a 20-foot-tall image on the movie screen. Those tiny blemishes and patches that we so casually ignore in daily life suddenly become huge boulders and gullies and strange markings of all kinds.

The Makeup Department has the job of making the Actors' faces acceptable to be seen as a 20-foot-tall image and still be gorgeous.

Time is another factor in hiring Makeup Department personnel. We never want to wait on set for an Actor to get into makeup. So it becomes imperative that we hire enough Makeup Artists and Hair Stylists to prevent that from happening, just as we did in the Wardrobe department.

Makeup Artists can be the unsung heroes of the show. They take the time in the morning with the Actors not only to do their makeup but also to put them in the proper frame of mind for the rest of the day. This can also work in reverse.   On one movie I was on, the Production Manager religiously shorted the crew's paychecks, sometimes refusing to pay their overtime. The makeup folk spent their time with the Actors in the morning complaining, and justly, about the paychecks. By the time the Actors walked onto the set they were so distraught that it took a half-hour of crew time to calm them.

3405 Body Makeup
The union requires that whenever a person must be made up higher up the arm than the wrists, and higher up the leg than the ankle, a qualified body makeup artist be hired to do that. In practice, we use our own discretion in terms of the body areas to be covered. Body makeup normally is done by a person of the same gender as the person being made up. We will need body makeup for scenes in which people are sunbathing on the beach or otherwise revealing more skin than usual.

Body Makeup Artists are hired only for the day needed and are not employed for the shooting length of the picture.

3406 Hair Stylists

Description	Amount	Units	X	Rate	Subtotal
Prep	0	Week	1	2,196.60	0
Shoot	4	Weeks	1	2,196.60	8,786
Wrap	0	Week	1	2,196.60	0
					8,786
Overtime allowance	10	%	1	0	0
Personal Equipment Rental	10	Weeks	1	0	0
Car Allowance	0	Week	1	0	0
Total					**8,786**

(BUDBOOK.MMB 2,671,976 • Category 3400 45,060 • Account 3406 8,786 • Cume: 0 • Change: 0)

Hair is very important to the look of a performer. Remember, without it the performer would be bald. There will be times when an Actor will have to have his or her hair dyed daily. Call times must be adjusted to compensate for this.

A TV show I was involved with recently had a dog and a man paired as a police team. The Executive Producer insisted on a screen test with the dog and the man to see if the "chemistry" between them was right for the show; that is, would the dog bite the man. On seeing the screen test the Producer decided that the dog and Actor worked out fine, but the dog was the wrong color. A Hair Stylist was hired to dye the dog a slightly lighter color per the Producer's request. Then another screen test was filmed to check the chemistry again. On this one, the dog just sat there and scratched, because the dye irritated its skin. The things we do for the sake of art!

3410 Makeup Supplies
We must budget for the sponges, pancake, and other makeup substances that will be used up during the course of filming.

3412 Wigs and Hairpieces
We need these items for many reasons – the most obvious one is that the stunt doubles seldom have the same hair color as the actors and have to wear wigs to look like them. Wigs can be expensive so we must be sure to budget accordingly.

3413 Special Makeup Design

Description	Amount	Units	X	Rate	Subtotal	
Designer - Prep	0		1	0	0	
Designer - Shoot	0		1	0	0	
Assistants	0		1	0	0	
Materials	0		1	0	0	
Work Space	0		1	0	0	
Equipment	0		1	0	0	
Lab Charges	0		1	0	0	
Total					**0**	

BUDBOOK.MMB 2,671,976
Category 3400 45,060
Account 3413 0
Cume: 0
Change: 0

We will use this account only when special makeup is necessary, as in science fiction shows. We must take care to schedule enough time for special makeup – on the series, *Planet of the Apes*, it took four hours every morning to make up each "monkey." We also must give our Makeup Designer plenty of time to prepare for the show, because prostheses and masks must be made to order for the show, usually in quantity, and each must be custom-designed for the Actor who will wear it.

3414 Prostheses

This job usually will fall to some people like The Burmans who have a long history of making good appliances and prostheses for the movie business. I know producers who tried to get away cheap a couple of times and spent more money correcting the errors than it would have taken to have the prosthesis made properly in the first place.

> **Prosthesis**: Usually an addition to someone, such as a fake arm or leg or false teeth. Prostheses, to work properly, must be designed well in advance of filming and tested on the actor, preferable on film (or tape), to see how it photographs. Something that looks good to the eye might look ridiculous on a large screen. If we are filming a horror epic it is essential that the Director and Makeup Artist together decide what look the creature will have. We might consult our Wardrobe Department as well in case a prosthesis extends down below the neckline, affecting the size of clothes.

It also is important to give the makeup folk the time necessary to build or fashion the devices to be worn. Casts of the actors must be made, and forms must be fitted to their faces or other parts of anatomy. As just stated, a little more money spent for a high-quality job here will save lots more money when we are filming and the false teeth don't fit and have to be reworked on the set.

3415 Special Appliances

"Appliances" usually refers to something someone wears; for instance in *Planet of the Apes,* when whole new heads were designed for the actors.

The makeup devices that fit over the actors' real heads are referred to as *appliances*.

3498 Other Charges
Makeup Tests
If we have special makeup or hair needs and we have to test them, we can't forget to budget for it.

Polaroid Camera/Film
One movie I worked in New York, the female lead insisted on her own Hair Stylist, a young man who had never worked in movies before. He did not understand continuity, and for the first two days he took the lady's wig home and restyled it at night. Her hair style changed from long shot to close-up in the same scene. Polaroid cameras can be useful in preventing this unhappy situation.

3500 Location Department

```
MMB Movie Magic Budgeting - [BUDBOOK.MMB -- 3500 -- Location Department]      _ ☐ ✕
MMB  File  Edit  Setup  Tools  Library  Go To  Magic  Window  Help            _ ☐ ✕
BUDBOOK.MMB          2,671,976    TOP SHEET                          Cume:        0
Category 3500           15,789    ACCOUNT                            Change:      0
                                  DETAIL
```

Acct#	Account Title	Page	Total
3501	Survey Costs	40	0
3502	Travel Costs	41	0
3503	Per Diem	41	0
3504	Lodging	41	0
3505	Meals	41	0
3506	Caterer	41	12,071
3507	Guards/Watchmen	42	0
3508	Police	42	0
3509	Firemen	42	0
3510	Local Contact	42	0
3511	Government Representative	42	0
3512	Site Rentals	42	0
3513	Location Offices	43	0
3514	Crew Mileage	43	0
3515	Shipping	43	0
3516	Customs Brokerage	44	0
3517	Passports/Visas	44	0
3518	Editing Facilities	44	0
3519	Dailies Screenings	44	0
3520	Heating/Air Conditioning	44	0

When I first started working in the movie business it was very difficult to film on location. The machinery of film making was very cumbersome. Today it is much simpler, although for some applications it is still practical to construct a set with wild walls and film in studio.

Wild walls: Walls that easily move away from the room to facilitate movement of cameras and lights.

Nowadays it is common to film on location. Studio filming is used only when necessary – for standing sets, for instance, or when special effects are needed.

Because of the increasing use of location vans (the original was the late, sorely lamented Cinemobile), very light self-blimped cameras, quartz lights, and Nagra portable tape recorders, location filming is the rule rather than the exception. Locations are always more realistic than sets; filming even in remote areas of foreign countries has become an everyday experience.

3501 Survey Costs

Description	Amount	Units	X	Rate	Subtotal
Travel	0		1	0	0
Accomodations	0		1	0	0
Per Diem	0		1	0	0
Car Rentals	0		1	0	0
Research Expenses	0		1	0	0
Entertainment	0		1	0	0
Still film/lab	0		1	0	0
Video Equipment	0		1	0	0
Video Cassettes	0		1	0	0
Telephones	0		1	0	0
Fax Charges	0		1	0	0
Gratuities	0		1	0	0
Local Contacts	0		1	0	0
Total					**0**

It is a very good idea, if you intend to go on location, to contact the local office of the Film Commission of the area to which you are going. All states, most large cities, and many foreign locations maintain film commissions whose purpose is to lure Hollywood to spend millions of dollars in the local economy. Many of these film commissions have offices in Los Angeles. A phone call could get you wonderfully idealized books of photos, lists of local talent and crews, and other devices to promote filming in that area. These can save us a lot of trouble in finding just the right location.

In Great Britain a survey is called a *recce* (pronounced "WRECK-ee"). The British have other amusing words for their movie business. I once asked Richard Lester if he needed a helicopter for a particular scene. He answered, "No, a zip-up will do." In my naive mind a zip-up is what happens after we – well – leave the set for a minute. In Britain a "zip-up" is what we call a parallel.

> **Parallel**: A system of platforms, built one on top of the other in increments usually of 6 feet, on which a camera crew and equipment can stand for filming.

Videotape Equipment

When we scout distant locations we must bring back with us some graphic representation of what we have seen. Videotape is ideal for this. Handy-cams are so small that they are little more trouble than still cameras. They can be rented for little money and easily pay for themselves in the convenience of showing art directors, producers, studio chiefs, cinematographers, and the rest what a location looks like. I recommend them highly.

Still Film and Lab

When we scout distant locations we must bring back with us some graphic representation of what we have seen. Still photographs also are ideal for this. Minoltas and Nikons are so small that they are no more trouble than video cameras. They can be rented, usually, for little money, and they easily pay for themselves in the convenience of showing art directors, producers, studio chiefs, cinematographers, and the rest what a location looks like. I recommend them highly.

3502 Travel Costs

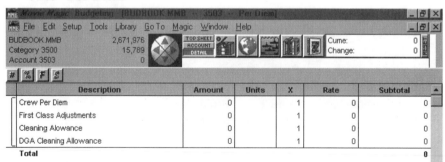

Description	Amount	Units	X	Rate	Subtotal	
To/From Locations	0		1	0	0	
First Class Adjustments	0		1	0	0	
Transport to Airports	0		1	0	0	
Excess Baggage Charges	0		1	0	0	
Gratuities	0		1	0	0	
Travel Insurance	0		1	0	0	
Total					**0**	

Remember that when we travel, not only our crew but also our equipment has to get to the location somehow. I have been able at times to travel very light and checked the equipment into the airport as excess baggage. Other times I have had to rent barges to ferry equipment, trucks, wardrobe, and so on, thousands of miles across oceans.

Also, be mindful that our contracts with certain of our crew and all our cast require first class transportation. Do not assume that they will waive this. Steerage is no fun for someone who is 6' 2" tall.

In some cases we contractually must provide for flight insurance. We also must be sure that our travelers fill out beneficiary cards before traveling, or else the benefits in case of accident would be paid to the producer instead of the proper heirs.

3503 Per Diem

Description	Amount	Units	X	Rate	Subtotal	
Crew Per Diem	0		1	0	0	
First Class Adjustments	0		1	0	0	
Cleaning Alowance	0		1	0	0	
DGA Cleaning Allowance	0		1	0	0	
Total					**0**	

> **Per Diem**: The money paid to crew and cast members to cover day-to-day expenses exclusive of the lodging, which the company pays for, and the location lunches, which the caterer provides. It usually consists of money for breakfast and dinner for six days, and breakfast, lunch and dinner for the seventh day. This price varies from city to city. In New York, obviously, it will be greater than in Newton, Massachusetts.
>
> Furthermore, the Directors Guild requires the company to pay all its members a cleaning allowance for each week spent on distant location.

3504 Lodging

Description	Amount	Units	X	Rate	Subtotal
Crew Lodging	0		1	0	0
First Class Adjustments	0		1	0	0
Hotel Gratuities	0		1	0	0
Apartment/Condo Rentals	0		1	0	0
House Rentals	0		1	0	0
Relocation Allowances	0		1	0	0
Total					**0**

BUDBOOK.MMB 2,671,976
Category 3500 15,789
Account 3504 0

Cume: 0
Change: 0

If the crew is to stay on distant location overnight, we have to provide them a place to sleep. For union members we will have to provide individual rooms for each crew and cast member. This brought about an amusing problem on a show I did. The Boom Operator was the wife of the Sound Mixer. I had to get a special waiver from the union for them to share a room.

Apartment/Condo Rental
When a show is shot over a long term, it is cost effective to rent apartments for those folks who are staying for several months, rather than let hotel bills chew into the budget. A nice apartment with a view and a microwave oven can cost as little as a third or a quarter of a suite in a moderate hotel. Local film commissions sometimes have lists of such places.

House Rental
In rare instances we contractually will have to provide a house for a star. This usually involves not only renting the house but also displacing a family, whom we will have to pay to be put up elsewhere. Try to avoid this if possible, but, when necessary, be sure to have budgeted not only for the rental but also for relocation of the displaced family.

3506 Caterer

Description	Amount	Units	X	Rate	Subtotal	
Cook/Driver - Local	4	Weeks	1	1,760.03	7,040	
Helper - Local	4	Weeks	1	982.8	3,931	
Extra Cook/Drivers	0		1	1,439.28	0	
Extra Helpers	0		1	982.8	0	
Overtime allowance	10	%	1	0	0	
					10,971	
Lunches - Local	20	Weeks	1	12.5	250	
Lunches - Distant	30	DistWks	1	12.5	375	
Dinners	50	Days	1	9.5	475	
Breakfasts	0		1	0	0	
Snacks	0		1	0	0	
Catering Unit	0		1	0	0	
Tables/Chairs/Setups	0		1	0	0	
Shelter	0		1	0	0	
Gas/Oil/Maintenance	0		1	0	0	
Total					**12,071**	

Window title: Movie Magic Budgeting - [BUDBOOK.MMB — 3506 — Caterer]
Menu: File Edit Setup Tools Library Go To Magic Window Help
BUDBOOK.MMB 2,671,976 Category 3500 15,789 Account 3506 12,071 Cume: 0 Change: 0

A caterer usually becomes the repository of all the ills of the company. I have hired few caterers who were able to keep everyone on the crew happy all the time. Most caterers who handle movie companies are really very respectable chefs who do an extremely difficult job very well in spite of the abuse they almost invariably get from the more dour crew members.

Try to remember a couple of guidelines here. The caterer should have more than one truck. If the caterer's only truck breaks down on the way to location, hiring another caterer on short notice can be a costly remedy. Also, in the choice of food, remember that some people eat only vegetarian meals or have other dietary requirements, so a good salad bar can solve a multitude of sins.

In budgeting, remember that we have to provide not only for the crew, cast, and extras, but also if we are working for a major producer guests will almost always appear at the location coincidentally with the lunch time, just to make sure that the show is going well. Also, if we are using someone's house as a location, it is politic to invite the family to lunch.

Furthermore, for budgeting purposes, we should remember to budget for a respectable percentage of "dinners" or second meals. About 30 percent of the time filming usually is about right unless the Director is out of control.

Breakfasts cannot be forgotten either. The cast members who arrive early for makeup and wardrobe, the makeup and wardrobe folks, and the drivers who drove the trucks in earliest of all, need to be fed. This can add up to as many as 25 people each day who get a free breakfast.

The six-hour rule: A state law which provides that an employer must give an employee a lunch break no later than six hours after work is begun, and a dinner break no later than six hours after the lunch break has finished. This is not in movie contracts, it is the law, and as an employer we must follow it.

When we have huge numbers of extras it is wise to hire two catering trucks to feed everyone in a timely fashion. The crew will eat a normal lunch; the second line for the extras can have equally good food but perhaps not so great a variety and, therefore, cost us less.

Enclosures
Remember that when we are feeding our crew on location we should try to keep them dry and warm or cool, when possible. I have rented tents for use during snowstorms in Colorado and during heat waves in the Mojave Desert.

3507 Guards
Most union contracts provide for a guarded parking lot for the Actors and crew during filming. Several excellent guard services cater to the movie industry. The important thing here is the presence of an actual human being to guard the cars, not a video camera.

3508 Police

Movie Magic Budgeting - [BUDBOOK.MMB - 3508 - Police]						_ 🗗 ✕
File Edit Setup Tools Library Go To Magic Window Help						_ 🗗 ✕
BUDBOOK.MMB 2,671,976			TOP SHEET / ACCOUNT / DETAIL		Cume:	0
Category 3500 15,789					Change:	0
Account 3508 0						

Description	Amount	Units	X	Rate	Subtotal	▲
Police Personnel	0	Day	1	398.58	0	
Overtime allowance	10	%	1	0	0	
Motorcycles	0	Day	1	30	0	
Cruisers	0		1	0	0	
Special Equipment	0		1	0	0	
Total					**0**	

The presence of uniformed officers on location reassures the local populace that we are legitimate and reassures the crew that the local populace probably won't become too rambunctious. Many cities require police officers to be present when filming on public property or even when we have our trucks parked on public property even though we are filming on private property. It is best to check with the local authorities for the local rules. And most cities that have seen filming before have a group of police officers used to working with movie companies.

Many cities, even New York City, charge nothing for the police officers who stay with us on location. We need them for traffic control, to help with running shots, and to keep the locals away from the equipment.

Los Angeles is still a bit retrograde, requiring us to hire off-duty police officers for these purposes.

Police Officers can be a great help in filming. I was out of town in a major city once and needed a traffic jam for a very long shot of the main character stuck in traffic. A local police officer told me exactly where to stall a car on the freeway to create the most beautiful traffic jam I ever saw. We got the shot in five minutes, moved our stalled car, and the jam was freed up in another five minutes, causing very little disruption of traffic.

3509 Fire Marshal

Any time we are filming in a location to which the public has access or whenever there is any sort of combustible material being filmed such as a lit fireplace, we will need a Fire Marshal present. That's the law. At least, we have to ask the Fire Department if a Fire Marshal is necessary and it will either assign one to us or not.

3510 Local Contact

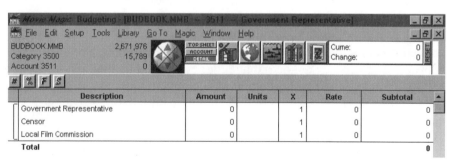

Description	Amount	Units	X	Rate	Subtotal
Prep	0	Week	1	0	0
Shoot	6	DistWks	1	0	0
Wrap	0	Week	1	0	0
Car Expenses	0		1	0	0
Telephone Expenses	0		1	0	0
Fax Expenses	0		1	0	0
Still Film/Lab	0		1	0	0
Total					**0**

Sometimes it is most valuable to hire a local resident who knows the streets, highways, buildings, and most important, the social structure of the town in which we are filming. We could find ourselves stepping on fewer toes that way.

3511 Government Representative

Description	Amount	Units	X	Rate	Subtotal
Government Representative	0		1	0	0
Censor	0		1	0	0
Local Film Commission	0		1	0	0
Total					**0**

Government Representative

In foreign countries, this person can be a great help in getting equipment, film, and personnel into and out of the country. Different countries have different laws governing this and generally it is helpful to try to obey the local laws.

Be aware when shipping equipment into a country for your own use and with the intent of shipping it home when finished, that a system, called a *carnet,* enables shipping such material into many countries without paying customs fees.

> **Carnet**: Customs declaration in which we solemnly swear that the materials we import into a country are for our own use, not for resale, and that we will return them to their point of origin when finished.

Censor

This usually is necessary only in foreign countries where there is some kind of government control or where the government is particularly sensitive to criticism for some reason. Those countries are becoming fewer and fewer, by the way.

3512 Site Rentals

```
Movie Magic Budgeting - [BUDBOOK.MMB — 3512 -- Site Rentals]         _ 🗗 ✕
File  Edit  Setup  Tools  Library  Go To  Magic  Window  Help         _ 🗗 ✕
BUDBOOK MMB          2,671,976    [TOP SHEET]                Cume:        0
Category 3500           15,789    [ACCOUNT]                  Change:      0
Account 3512                 0    [DETAIL]
```

Description	Amount	Units	X	Rate	Subtotal
Daily Rates	0		1	0	0
Prep/Rig/Dress	0		1	0	0
Hold Days	0		1	0	0
Cleanup	0		1	0	0
Residents Relocation	0		1	0	0
Animal Kennels	0		1	0	0
Street Permits	0		1	0	0
Crew Parking	0		1	0	0
Equipment Parking	0		1	0	0
Lunch Site	0		1	0	0
Location Gratuities	0		1	0	0
Permits and Fees	0		1	0	0
Special Effects Permits	0		1	0	0
Total					**0**

Site rentals can vary widely from place to place, from a few kroner or zlotys to thousands of dollars. On a recent production, a sequel to an earlier show, we needed the same house that had been established in the earlier show. The owners saw us coming and charged $4,000 per day. We also had to put them up in the best hotel in the city, after they had returned from their fully paid vacation at our expense.

On the other hand, I was filming once in Montpelier, Vermont; the owner of a large mansion, bless her, wanted to pay me to use her house in the film.

We must remember that each location requires several areas of operation: the actual set itself, production truck parking, street access, crew parking, a crew lunch area, street and business permits.

Street Permits
Almost any local government wrings its hands in glee at the approach of a filming company. The street permits alone usually will support one or two local services for a few months. Furthermore, a study conducted by a local government on one of my distant locations calculated that because of the extensive use of local facilities, each dollar spent by a movie company on location is multiplied in the local economy by a factor of 5. In other words, we hire a local Caterer. The Caterer hires extra help for our show. The extra help have more money to spend in the local economy, giving more local people jobs, and so forth. This multiplies the effect of our presence on the local economy.

Los Angeles City, County, and California State maintain an office in Hollywood that would be overjoyed to supply us with information about filming on the streets here, including street permit fees, police requirements, and so forth.

Crew Parking
Crews must have a place to park. In some cases a guard is needed in the parking area so crews do not worry about having cars broken into. Normally the location manager will arrange for a large enough parking lot to accommodate crew vehicles, production van, equipment trucks, and still have room left over to serve the crew lunch. It doesn't have to be as large as Kansas, Rhode Island will do.

Street Parking
Our permit should enable us to keep our necessary equipment as close as possible to the set. If we are filming in a house and the crew and trucks are parked a block away down the street, it is advisable to try to permit at least the camera truck for street parking, because the Camera Assistants will be running back and forth to it every few minutes for lenses and such. The ideal situation, of course, is to film in a building in the middle of a large parking lot.

Lunch Site
The cast and crew members have to eat somewhere. I remember filming a show in Chicago when the Location Manager forgot to arrange for a lunch site and it was snowing outside. I got lucky. Next door was an unused bank building. The caretaker balked at first, but eventually the thought of a free lunch and being around all those movie stars persuaded him.

Location Gratuities

We also will be spending more money from this account in other areas. For instance, suppose we are filming at 3:00 AM in the middle of a wheat field in Kansas and the next-door neighbor suddenly appears and fires up a power lawn mower. Does this person want to mow the lawn? No, the gardener wants some of those location gratuities.

Kennel

No matter where we film, even in Point Barrow, Alaska, there will always be a next door neighbor whose dog barks incessantly. We have to pay to have the cur kenneled while we shoot. Of course, we could loop the whole scene, which is probably much more expensive.

Repair

Our location agreement probably reads that when we have finished filming in a particular location we must return it to its former condition. Several companies in Los Angeles specialize in handling the little nicks and scratches in balustrades and antique furniture for movie companies. We also could have the Art Department handle the problem. Either way, it is wise to cooperate with the owner as much as practicable to restore the location because another film company may wish to use the same location next week or we may want to go back for retakes.

3513 Location Offices

After we have put up the crew in a hotel, we will want a base of operations for ourselves. Sometimes just one large room will serve as a headquarters for everyone, and sometimes we take a corridor of the hotel with several adjacent rooms for the various departments.

Mobile Office

At times I have rented an entire mobile office, consisting of a motor home or converted bus decked out with desks, copiers, fax machines, computers, portable phones, and even a conference room.

3514 Crew Mileage

If crew and cast members must drive daily to a distant location, they will request reimbursement for the use of their vehicles. Contractually we have to reimburse our cast and DGA members at $0.30 per mile, ($0.31 for DGA). We pay teamsters not only mileage but also rental for their autos on a per-week basis.

3515 Shipping

Description	Amount	Units	X	Rate	Subtotal
Film Shipping	0		1	0	0
Airport Pickup/Delivery	0		1	0	0
Equipment Shipping	0		1	0	0
Pickup/Delivery	0		1	0	0
Crating/Packing	0		1	0	0
Load/Unload Labor	0		1	0	0
Export Taxes	0		1	0	0
Total					**0**

If we have huge amounts of equipment, we may wish to ship it instead of taking it as overweight luggage. Shipping overseas can be amusing. I had to ship a 40-foot trailer, filled to the rafters with equipment containers, to a Caribbean Island for a location shoot. The only possible route was to have the trailer shipped from Florida to one island, offloaded, and shipped by barge to the location, the location's docks being too small to handle the normal container ship. The stopover proved to be troublesome. A local customs officer insisted that the truck be opened and every single equipment container opened and the contents verified against the waybill before releasing it for the location. This threatened to hold us up for a week. Amazing what a case of good rum will do for international relations!

We must remember that, in shipping, the items not only must be shipped but also must get to the airport for shipping, and be picked up from the airport and transported to the location, so those costs must be figured in.

3516 Customs Fees
It is advisable to contact a reputable customs brokerage firm if filming on foreign soil. Customs fees vary widely from place to place, and we do not wish to be caught short.

3517 Passports and Visas

Description	Amount	Units	X	Rate	Subtotal
Passports	0		1	10	0
Visas	0		1	0	0
Medical Costs	0		1	0	0
Foreign Work Permits	0		1	0	0
Total					**0**

Passports

It usually takes two weeks to obtain a passport from the State Department. We can request a rush order, which could mean next day or two day service, but most of us just keep our passports up to date, looking with dismay at our changing passport pictures as they are updated every few years.

Visas

Sometimes it is necessary to obtain travel visas to enter a foreign country. The local consulate should be contacted as soon as possible when we know we are going, to give it time to do the bureaucratic thing. To travel to some countries it may be necessary for us to obtain other papers as well

Medical Exams

These can be gotten from any reputable doctor. We may also need to have inoculations against certain diseases.

Foreign Work Permits

In some countries, Canada, for example, it is necessary to obtain work permits for ourselves and the cast and crew members to film. Some countries insist that we hire a certain percentage of native workers for the film; others just want our income. We must check with the local consulate for the rules specific to the country in which we will be filming.

Interestingly enough, a friend of mine was scouting a foreign country in which his grandparents had been born. The first night there, my friend was arrested by the local militia and told that because his grandparents were born there he was considered a native and he was being drafted into the army. (Amazing what a case of good rum . . .)

3520 Heating and Air Conditioning

At times we need to hire an air conditioning service for the comfort of the actors and the crew. I was filming in a state prison during the heat of the summer with a couple of actors who were over 70 years old. The silly state authorities had forgotten to install air conditioning for the inmates. I brought out a unit from Los Angeles that air conditioned a whole wing of the building so our actors could work in some kind of comfort. The inmates of that wing were sorry to see us wrap.

When filming outside during the coldest part of Winter, we will want to rent space heaters for the crew and extras to huddle around between shots. We just have to be aware of the usual safety precautions for such devices.

3521 Location Weather Service

A few good nation wide weather services can give accurate predictions, for the next few hours anyway. If we need a weather report immediately and have no such service, phoning the local airport and asking for cloud cover for the next few hours will give us a short-term prediction, but we can't do that more than once or twice because eventually they catch on that we aren't flying Piper Apaches after all.

3600 Transportation Department

Movie Magic Budgeting - [BUDBOOK.MMB - 3600 - Transportation Department]

File Edit Setup Tools Library GoTo Magic Window Help

BUDBOOK.MMB 2,671,976
Category 3600 30,671

Cume: 0
Change: 0

Acct#	Account Title	Page	Total
3601	Transportation Coord.	45	8,000
3602	Transportation Captain	45	8,116
3603	Dispatcher	45	0
3604	Mechanic	45	0
3605	Drivers	45	0
3606	Picture Vehicles	46	0
3607	Production Vehicles	47	7,040
3608	Personnel Vehicles	48	0
3609	Self-drive Rentals	48	0
3610	Pickup/Delivery Charges	48	0
3611	Gas/Oil/Maintenance	48	0
3612	Trucks to Location	48	0
3613	Vehicle Preparation	49	0
3614	Special Equipment	49	0
3615	Stunt Vehicles	49	0
3616	Office Expenses	49	0
3617	Overtime for drivers	49	0
3697	Loss & Damage	49	0
3698	Miscellaneous	49	0
3699	**Total Fringes**		**7,515**

The Transportation Department is one of the most crucial areas of the budget – definitely not to be taken for granted.

Whenever we have a department prepping or wrapping, picking up or delivering items such as wardrobe or set dressing, a truck and a driver are needed to handle that chore. So our transport folks will need prep and wrap time to accommodate the needs of each department.

One more important thing; the driver of each vehicle needs a federal driver's license for the vehicle he or she is driving. If the driver lacks the license and gets into an accident, our insurance will be void. So we must be sure to check each driver's license to see if it's a Class A, Class B, or Class C license, and allow that driver to drive only the trucks for which he or she is licensed. Furthermore, copies of all the relevant drivers licenses should be kept in the production office in case OSHA decides to check on us.

3601   Transportation Coordinator

Description	Amount	Units	X	Rate	Subtotal
Prep	0	Week	1	2,000	0
Shoot	4	Weeks	1	2,000	8,000
Wrap	0	Week	1	2,000	0
					Excluded
Overtime allowance	10	%	1	0	0
Personal Equipment Rental	0	Week	1	0	0
Car Rental	10	Weeks	1	0	0
Total					**8,000**

(Window info: BUDBOOK.MMB 2,671,976, Category 3600 30,871, Account 3601 8,000; Cume: 0, Change: 0)

This person heads the Transportation Department, the person who keeps things running smoothly. As a UPM I always try to hire a Transportation Coordinator as soon as possible, because the job is very large. The coordinator has to hire all the other the drivers, assign them to the proper trucks, and oversee the maintenance of those trucks. If we have several locations spread widely apart, we might hire one Transportation Captain for each.

On *Days Of Thunder*, in which there was a whole picture car unit all by itself, the excellent John Feinblatt coordinated just the picture cars under the aegis of the overall coordinator, David Marder. His budget for that film was greater than most low-budget movies.

3603   Dispatcher
During *War and Remembrance* we hired a dispatcher who stayed in the office and kept track of each truck and driver, where they were, when they would return, and so on. It saved a lot of guesswork. Each driver checked in and out with the dispatcher whenever going anywhere.

3604   Mechanic
Whenever we photograph cars that have to be kept in good running condition is it wise to hire a mechanic as a driver, pay a little extra, and let this person keep the picture cars in good running condition. On *The Man Who Broke 1000 Chains,* one scene featured two dozen or so cars from the 1920s. We also had three mechanics who knew how to keep them running. The painful part was when they stalled and had to be crank started. As First A.D., I usually was standing next to them, and at the end of that day I had an extremely sore right arm and back.

3605 Picture Vehicles

Description	Amount	Units	X	Rate	Subtotal	
Taxis	0		1	0	0	
Limousines (Driv. Incl)	0	Hour	1	0	0	
Busses	0		1	0	0	
Police Vehicles	0		1	0	0	
Ambulances	0		1	0	0	
Coroner's Wagons	0		1	0	0	
Fire Equipment	0		1	0	0	
Trucks/Vans	0		1	0	0	
SWAT Trucks	0		1	0	0	
Trailers	0		1	0	0	
Military Equipment	0		1	0	0	
Construction Equipment	0		1	0	0	
Motorcycles	0		1	0	0	
Stagecoaches	0		1	0	0	
Wagons/Rigs	0		1	0	0	
Principals' Cars	0		1	0	0	
TV Mini-Cams	0		1	0	0	
Armored Trucks	0		1	0	0	
Utility Trucks	0		1	0	0	

There are many kinds of picture vehicles. In broad strokes, a picture vehicle is anything in front of the camera with wheels that rolls and carries a person or things.

Just to point out some of the problems connected with picture vehicles, witness the scene of the battle of El Alamein from *War and Remembrance*. We needed World War II vehicles from Germany, Italy, America and Britain. Enough vehicles to cover maybe two or three acres. We contacted every antique war vehicle club in the United States and put out the word that we needed the vehicles for the scene. Dozens of collectors responded. Many of the vehicles were the right vintage but the wrong color. Many were not working models and could not travel under their own power. But whatever the state, we collected several dozen of them. This entailed paying the owners to have the vehicles transported to the location in the Mojave Desert. We had to put up the owners in hotels and motels throughout their travel to and from the location, as well as pay for food and gasoline. For those large vehicles that had to be trailered, we paid for the trailer rental. Most German Panzer tanks are not licensed to travel down the interstate highways. And on the trailers they had to be covered by tarpaulins because they would have attracted too much attention during the trip. We had to pay for the tarps.

After the vehicles, tanks, ferrets, motorcycles, armored personnel carriers, half-tracks, dozens of them, had arrived on location we had to hire a crew to repaint them the proper desert camouflage colors, in what we call peel paint.

Peel-Paint: A kind of paint that, after it dries, turns into a plastic skin that can be pulled right off the object painted, making it unnecessary to use paint remover. The movie industry uses it for temporary paint jobs.

During filming we had to feed and lodge the vehicles' owners and their mechanics. When we finished the scene, we restored all the vehicles to their original colors again at our expense before they were returned to wherever they came from. As we can see, this scene cost a small fortune just for the picture vehicles.

Stagecoaches and Wagon Rigs

Stagecoaches and wagon rigs belong in the transportation department. They have wheels and carry things, right?

Description	Amount	Units	X	Rate	Subtotal
Airplanes:	0		1	0	0
Fuel	0		1	0	0
Pilots	0		1	0	0
Co-Pilots	0		1	0	0
Ground Crew	0		1	0	0
Fuel Trucks	0		1	0	0
Landing Permits	0		1	0	0

(Movie Magic Budgeting - [BUDBOOK.MMB - 3606 - Picture Vehicles]; File Edit Setup Tools Library Go To Magic Window Help; BUDBOOK.MMB 2,671,976 Category 3600 30,671 Account 3606 0; Cume: 0 Change: 0)

Airplanes

Airplanes have their own problems. Usually we have to hire someone to fly them. And they need fuel and maintenance. If we are filming on a public airfield, we need to pay for landing permits as well.

With planes and helicopters we are well served to contact a professional in the field and let this person handle the entire aerial photography end for us. Such people will arrange for the planes, pilots, cameras, and everything in a package situation.

Any number of excellent antique airplane museums keep working models around, and organizations such as the Confederate Air Force or the Producers' Air Force will help us put together a whole flotilla of planes if we wish. Just remember that older planes are far less reliable than newer ones, and sometimes they don't take off when we wish them to.

On the other hand, if we need a new airliner for our show, airliner mock-ups are available for filming at laughably low prices, complete with cabins, cockpits, galleys, everything that a respectable airliner would have, all with wild walls, and they are already in studios in the city, just waiting for us to photograph them.

Furthermore, the U.S. Air Force has a liaison office in Los Angeles which is prepared and eager to help producers use Air Force facilities to make their shows more technologically correct.

Description	Amount	Units	X	Rate	Subtotal	
Helicopters:	0		1	0	0	
Fuel	0		1	0	0	
Pilots	0		1	0	0	
Co-Pilots	0		1	0	0	
Ground Safety Officers	0		1	0	0	
Night Lights	0	Day	1	400	0	
Fuel Trucks	0		1	0	0	
Landing Permits	0		1	0	0	
					0	

Helicopters

Helicopters require special budgetary treatment. In addition to the regular considerations, we must provide for a ground safety officer and night lights, if the chopper is to land after dark near our location. The chopper usually will have its own fuel truck and mechanic, which will be on location to help out.

Filming helicopters requires special attention to rehearsal and safety meeting standards. Choppers have traditionally been "fun" for the crew, and everyone wants to take a ride in the thing. But more accidents have happened with choppers due to ignorance of safety rules than almost any other object except cars. One well-known director died when he was thinking about a scene and absent mindedly walked into the rotor blade.

Description	Amount	Units	X	Rate	Subtotal	
Trains:	0		1	0	0	
Fuel	0		1	0	0	
Crew	0		1	0	0	
Right-of-way Permits	0		1	0	0	

Trains

The use of trains will give us great visual value, but also tremendous logistical problems. We can't forget that, when we want Take 2, the train can't just stop and back up to first position. It takes time to stop, time to back up, and time to reset for the second take.

On *Butch and Sundance, the Early Days* we hired the Cumbres and Toltec narrow-gauge railroad for our train robbery. It was March when we filmed and the railroad had been out of use since the previous October. We had to hire a crew to get the train out of its winter mothballs, oil and lube it, fire it up and test it. This took the better part of two weeks. Then we had to rent a special train to clear the snow off the tracks so we could move it to where we wanted to photograph it. While we were photographing it, we added the train crew to our payroll and fed and lodged them with our crew. And all this time, we were paying for the right-of-way, because the railroad tracks are not always owned by the railroad that owns the train. It was sort of like renting a car and driving it on a toll road. When we finished filming with the train, we paid to have it returned to its shed and re-mothballed.

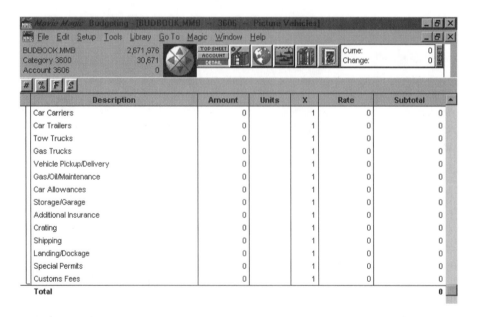

Boats

Boats likewise have special problems. If we are to film boats on open water we will need to purchase extra hull insurance, for instance. And do not forget the ubiquitous docking fees.

Description	Amount	Units	X	Rate	Subtotal
Car Carriers	0		1	0	0
Car Trailers	0		1	0	0
Tow Trucks	0		1	0	0
Gas Trucks	0		1	0	0
Vehicle Pickup/Delivery	0		1	0	0
Gas/Oil/Maintenance	0		1	0	0
Car Allowances	0		1	0	0
Storage/Garage	0		1	0	0
Additional Insurance	0		1	0	0
Crating	0		1	0	0
Shipping	0		1	0	0
Landing/Dockage	0		1	0	0
Special Permits	0		1	0	0
Customs Fees	0		1	0	0
Total					**0**

Obviously using a picture vehicle entails far more than merely renting a car and filming it. If the car is required to do stunts, for instance, we must first strengthen the chassis and body to enable the stunts to happen, then possibly build a roll-cage into the body in case the car flips during the stunt. If the car is to be photographed with outriggers or car mounts, it is wise to stiffen the shock absorbers to provide a steadier ride and lower the air pressure in the tires to allow for a softer ride.

3607 Production Vehicles

Description	Amount	Units	X	Rate	Subtotal
Production Van:	0		1	0	0
Travel	0		1	0	0
Shoot	10	Weeks	1	0	0
Driver:	0		1	0	0
Prep	0	Week	1	1,760.03	0
Shoot	4	Weeks	1	1,760.03	7,040
Wrap	0	Week	1	1,760.03	0
	0		1	0	0
Camera Truck:	0		1	0	0
Grip Truck:	0		1	0	0
Electric Truck:	0		1	0	0
Prop Truck:	0		1	0	0
Prop Wagon:	0		1	0	0
Set Dressing Truck:	0		1	0	0
Set Dressing Wagon:	0		1	0	0
Construction Truck:	0		1	0	0
Construction Crew Cab	0		1	0	0
Honeywagon #1:	0		1	0	0

The vehicles that carry crew members and equipment from one location to another are called *production vehicles*. Several things must be considered here: Each truck must have a driver. Each truck must have fuel. Each department that has things to rent or buy and return, must have a truck to do so, and each of these must have sufficient time for prepping and wrapping the show.

Production Van

The biggest vehicle on any location almost always is the production van. This is usually a 40-foot trailer that carries all the equipment for the entire Electric and Grip Departments, including lights, cables, and stands. Some production vans have a small office in the front of the trailer for those departments to do their paperwork.

On the back of the tractor section, in place of what would normally be a small bunkbed arrangement for the driver, are two 750-amp generators (or 1000-amp for the bigger rigs). The driver sometimes doubles as generator operator, especially if he or she owns the rig.

The procedure is to park the trailer as close to the set as possible without it being in the background of any of the shots, remove the tractor and prop up the trailer on jacks, and keep the tractor with the generators right next to the set. The generators will be very quiet, so they can be close to the set.

The production van needs some prep and wrap time. The electricians and grips not only must load and unload it before and after filming but also rearrange the shelving in the trailer to accommodate our particular package of equipment. This takes time and personnel.

The original production van, the Cinemobile, was invented by a genius, Fouad Said, the Cinematographer of the old *I Spy* TV series with Bill Cosby. It is sorely missed.

Camera Truck

The second most important truck in the stable is the camera truck. This usually is a cube van, something like a postal service van, with interior shelving that can be customized for the camera package. The sound package also travels in this vehicle.

Two special items are on this vehicle. The first is a light tight room that the Assistant Cameraman can use as a darkroom. This needs only a small amount of space with a shelf large enough to hold the magazine and some film and enough space to stand. The important part is that it be light tight. The second is a power supply because the sound equipment includes walkie-talkies. These must be recharged every night in this van. So we need a small generator or a goodly number of industrial batteries.

The Camera Truck usually is parked very close to the set so the Assistant Cameramen do not have to run far for special lenses and equipment.

Grip and Electric Trucks

We need the grip and electric trucks only if we have no production van. When I was filming *Bananas* in San Juan, Puerto Rico, we needed grip and electric trucks because the streets of Old San Juan were too narrow for our production van to turn corners, so we split the departments into separate smaller trucks that maneuvered with far more agility.

Prop Truck

A few Property Masters have prop "boxes" that are 40-foot trailers. The company provides the tractor and driver. Otherwise, the company sends the prop truck to make pickups at the property rental houses and also picks up the prop boxes from the Prop Master's house and fastens them to the walls of the prop truck so they become almost like built ins.

Prop Wagon

The Prop Department will need to make pickups and deliveries during the course of filming. Because the prop truck is needed on the set all the time, a wagon can do this. If possible, the wagon can be shared by two or three departments for pickups, such as set dressing and props, or sometimes wardrobe.

Set Dressing Truck

If there is little enough set dressing, we will try to fit it onto the prop truck. For a big show, however, a separate truck will be needed.

Construction Truck

If the show requires considerable construction, we may have to hire two or three trucks to handle it. On *War and Remembrance* we had a whole Transportation Division just for the Construction Department, with its own captain, dispatcher, and phone lines. But that's an outrageous example.

Construction Crew Cab

Crew cabs are elongated pickup trucks that have a back seat for more crew members and an oversize bed for carrying large objects. They serve many departments and can move things quickly over short distances. Usually one of the crew cabs on location has a huge gasoline tank with a pump built into the bed; this will service the trucks while we are filming so that the drivers need not stop at a gasoline station after work on overtime.

Honeywagons

Honeywagons are the long tractor-trailer combinations that have six or seven dressing rooms built into them as well as restrooms for the crew. The SAG contract provides that each member of the cast have an individual dressing room, not shared with another actor. Sometimes if we schedule the program properly, we can have one Actor finish up in the morning and another Actor called to the set just after lunch; these can share a dressing room because they are not there at the same time.

If an Actor's contract provides for a large dressing room, sometimes that Actor will be satisfied with a double room made from two single rooms in the honeywagon from which the intervening wall has been removed.

Description	Amount	Units	X	Rate	Subtotal
Honeywagon #2:	0		1	0	0
Wardrobe Truck	0		1	0	0
Wardrobe Wagon:	0		1	0	0
Crew Cabs:	0		1	0	0
MiniVans:	0		1	0	0
Busses:	0		1	0	0
Insert Car	0		1	0	0
Water Truck	0		1	0	0
Utility Trucks	0		1	0	0
Station Wagons:	0		1	0	0
Motor Homes:	0		1	0	0
Stake Bed Truck	0		1	0	0
	0		1	0	0
Star Trailers	0		1	0	0
	0		1	0	0
Wardrobe Trailers	0		1	0	0
	0		1	0	0
Makeup Trailers	0		1	0	0
Total					**7.040**

Wardrobe Truck

On *War and Remembrance* we hired a 40-foot trailer into which we installed washing machines, ironing boards, sewing machines, mannequins – all the trappings of a complete traveling Wardrobe Department. There also were double rows of clothing racks reaching from floor to ceiling in two tiers for all the military uniforms we needed, as well as period clothing for the extras.

MiniVans

Minivans are good for scouting locations with large numbers of people. Some of the newer ones have cell phones built in, although most production people carry cell phones anyway.

Busses

Union contracts provide that a crew member can report to one location, but if the crew must travel to another location during the day busses must be provided. And at the end of the day the crew members must be bussed back to where their cars are.

Insert Car

This is a highly specialized vehicle hired only for running shots with the actors having dialogue inside a moving vehicle. Insert cars are large rebodied pickup trucks that have a gymnasium of pipes and wires arranged about the truck bed on which cameras and lights can be attached. They also carry a small generator to power the lights and camera and, of course, a tow bar from which to tow the picture vehicle.

Towing the vehicle takes the responsibility of driving out of the hands of the actors, who already have plenty to do saying their lines, acting, slating their own takes, and trying to see around the bright lights shining through the windshield at them.

Water Truck

Whenever we film in an area with dirt roads or in the middle of a field, we will want a water truck to suppress the dust. Dust gets into everything – cameras, lights, vehicles, makeup – and causes all sorts of problems. The water truck can keep the dirt watered down so dust can't fly about.

Motor Homes

Most likely the major actors will want to have motor homes. This must be contractual or else we are not obligated to supply them. Here's an easy way to get around this problem: First, find out if the Actor would agree to a double room in the Honeywagon. If that fails, ask if the Actor will agree to a star trailer. This has definite advantages. We can haul it to location, use one of the crew cabs, dismount it, and use the crew cab for runs during the day, so we don't lose the service of a driver. Trailers are easily as luxurious as motor homes and require far less maintenance. What the Actor doesn't like is that the Driver of a motor home becomes something like a valet, doing personal errands during the shooting day. By using a trailer, the Driver is lost to the Actor. But most actors I know will gladly settle for a trailer rather than a motor home. Explain that the Actor will have more privacy to study his or her lines, because the driver won't be hanging around all day.

Makeup Trailer

Normally the Makeup Department will set up shop in a specially designed makeup trailer. These trailers come complete with running water in sinks designed for washing hair, mirrors surrounded by light bulbs – all the comforts of a studio Makeup Department.

Wardrobe Trailer

If we didn't lease a traveling wardrobe trailer with all the builtins from our Wardrobe Supervisor, there are wardrobe trailers for hire with room for only racks of clothes, or entire setups with cleaning machines and the like, or anything between.

3607 Personnel Vehicles

We might need cars or other vehicles to pick up Actors and the Director prior to filming, drive them to location, and return them to home at wrap time. If it sounds like a luxury, just consider this: The Director still has to see dailies and have conferences with the Editor and Producer after wrap time. And sometime between then and tomorrow morning he or she has to study the script pages for tomorrow's filming and fix the shot plot in his or her head. Any extra time the Director can steal from the 24-hour day is well worth it. And sometimes being driven to and from the set affords another hour of day time to work.

I also worked with one major star who was very tall. He worked for an average of 14 hours per day. We had a Driver pick him up in the early morning (5:00 AM or so) and return him home in the evening (8:00 PM or so) in a van that had the rear seats replaced by a mattress so he could nap to and from the set.

3609 Self-Drive Rentals

This is a duplication from the Location Department. Normally, when filming in Los Angeles, we must rent no cars. However, at times, such as when we have flown in an Actor from another city, we may have to pick up the car rental for the person.

At times it will be more to our advantage to lease a car on a long-term basis, rather than pay someone mileage or rent that person's own car from them. If our car rental and mileage bill works out to over $500/month and it costs us $450 to lease a car and buy the gasoline, the choice is obvious. I suggested that to one major company which was renting my car from me for months at a time but the company had a policy which prevented it. They felt silly, and I had a few good dinners.

3610 Pick-up and Delivery Charges

At times we may have to arrange for vehicles to be brought to where we are.

3611 Gas, Oil, and Maintenance

We better not forget this account. It will cost us dearly if there is no money for gasoline and oil.

Part of this also is the safety requirement. At least once every day the Driver of each truck must do a "walkaround," checking all the reservoirs and cables for leaks or damage, checking the brake pads and lights – all the safety requirements. The driver must sign a paper every day stating that the walkaround was accomplished. Should there be an accident, OSHA will want to see that every precaution was taken to prevent the accident, and that paper will be part of the proof that we were mindful of all the safety rules.

3612 Trucks to Location

Magic Magic Budgeting - [BUDBOOK.MMB - 3612 - Trucks to Location]						_ 日 X
File Edit Setup Tools Library Go To Magic Window Help						_ 日 X

BUDBOOK.MMB	2,671,976		TOP SHEET ACCOUNT DETAIL		Cume:	0
Category 3600	30,671				Change:	0
Account 3612	0					

Description	Amount	Units	X	Rate	Subtotal	
Drivers	0	1		0	0	
Garage	0	1		0	0	
Lodging	0	1		0	0	
Per Diem	0	1		0	0	
Tolls, Expenses	0	1		0	0	
Fuel	0	1		0	0	
Maintenance	0	1		0	0	
Total					**0**	

When we film on a distant location, where the crew has to be put up in a hotel for one night or more, we have to pay to get our trucks there with the equipment, props, and so forth. If it is a long drive, the Drivers will need money for food and shelter during the trip as well.

And sometimes we will have unexpected expenses. I filmed one movie in a distant location and the Driver of the wardrobe truck hadn't had his eyeglasses checked recently and did not read the "overhang" sign correctly on a bridge crossing the Interstate. He neatly peeled back the roof of the whole front half of a 40-foot trailer. We had to pay for the repair, as well as getting out a new trailer immediately to finish driving the wardrobe to the location.

3613 Vehicle Preparation

Picture cars seldom can be used exactly the way they reach us. Sometimes, they have to be painted. Sometimes, they have to be strengthened for stunts. Sometimes, the attachments for outriggers have to be welded to the chassis, which has to be strengthened to accept them.

Outriggers: Picture vehicles which are used over a long period of time, as for instance the Pontiac Firebirds of *The Rockford Files*, usually are rigged with outriggers to make filming easier. Outriggers are platforms that can be attached to either side of the vehicle, or the front, with steel tubes that fit into slots in the chassis and are held there by bolts. The camera,

Operator, and an Assistant can stand on these platforms and photograph the car occupants while the car is in motion. The car chassis has been strengthened so the car doesn't "lean" due to the excess weight.

If a car window or windshield must be knocked out during filming, the glass will have to be made of candy glass for the event. Regular car glass has been specially treated to withstand tremendous blows by everything from hammers to baseball bats, to protect the safety of the occupants. So we need movie FX glass to break on cue.

We also may have to set a car on fire for the picture. All cars today are made almost exclusively with fire-retardant materials, so our Special Effects crew will have to rig the car with a propane bottle and squibs. This must be done well ahead of the filming.

3614 Special Equipment

Description	Amount	Units	X	Rate	Subtotal
Scissors Lifts	0		1	0	0
Condors	0		1	0	0
Cherry Pickers	0		1	0	0
Total					**0**

Different filming circumstances require different vehicles. A scissors lift or cherry picker might make a dandy platform for a large lamp to emulate moonlight for our scene.

3700 Videotape Production

Acct#	Account Title	Page	Total
3701	Playback Operator	50	0
3702	Playback Assistant	50	0
3703	Video Playback Package	50	0
3704	Teleprompters	50	0
3705	Production Unit	50	0
3706	Video Display	51	0
3707	Video RawStock	51	0
3797	Loss & Damage	51	0
3798	Miscellaneous	51	0
3799	**Total Fringes**		**0**
	Total		**0**

If we are shooting our entire show on videotape, we need to pay attention to this category; otherwise, not necessarily. We'll go through the accounts anyway, but if videotape is involved, the best plan is to find a reliable videotape production house with a state-of-the-art production van and bid out the job. Each production house has its own modus operandi, its own equipment, and each will swear that this is the best there is.

Videotape plays an increasing role in film production. Eventually, this section will be capable of handling an entire production shot on videotape. For now, it is still a compendium of film shooting and tape or digital editing. Watch for expansions in future releases.

Suffice it to say that videotape is an electronic medium, whereas film is a chemical medium. The images on film are evident; on videotape, they are latent and must be made evident by an electronic viewing process – much to the dismay of one director who shot his show on tape and then held it up to the light to see the image!

This already is a factor in much of post-production, as noted earlier. It will be a greater factor in the future with the inevitable evolution of technologies such as HDTV and DVD. For this reason true understanding of video production budgeting is important to the filmmaker.

In very broad strokes, the systems are the same. One still must have an apparatus for capturing the image, and the medium on which the image is captured must be transferred to another medium to be manipulated for editing.

Film is far more suitable for projection in theaters, having a much more highly defined image. Tape is far more convenient to photograph, as one can immediately replay what has been shot and see if the take is acceptable. Of course, HDTV, in which the scan lines are so small as to be almost nonexistent, could change all of this.

In editing tape is far more convenient to work with, and digital editing is more convenient still.

3701-03 Video Playback

We use this account only if we have video playback, as in having a prop TV set on the set that must show a TV show. This is a duplicate of these items in the Property category.

3704 Teleprompters

Description	Amount	Units	X	Rate	Subtotal
Operator:	0		1	0	0
Prep	0	Week	1	0	0
Shoot	4	Weeks	1	0	0
Wrap	0	Week	1	0	0
					0
Personal Equipment Rental	10	Weeks	1	0	0
Car Allowance	0	Week	1	0	0
Supplies	0		1	0	0
Crawl Typing	0		1	0	0
Delivery/Shipping	0		1	0	0
Misc. Charges	0		1	0	0
Total					**0**

A teleprompter is a large box placed in front of the camera lens with a one-way mirror device inside of it, on which the dialogue is projected to allow the Actor to read his or her lines while looking directly into the camera.

Teleprompters were invented to help newscasters broadcast the news while looking directly into the camera, which makes them look sincere and enables us to believe what they are saying. For some reason, the TV stations still insist that newscasters shuffle papers on the desk in front of them, even though it is perfectly obvious that they are not using the papers on the desk to do anything more than shuffle during commercials. Yet shuffle they do.

You will always find the Actor who, out of confusion, memory dropout, or just bad manners, cannot or will not memorize lines. Teleprompters cater to those unfortunates. In this case the teleprompter screen can be placed anywhere in the set in plain sight of the Actor but out of sight of the camera and usually in such a way that the Actor appears to be speaking the lines to someone else.

We must remember that if a teleprompter is to be used, we have to get the copy to the teleprompt typist well in advance of the filming. It's not fun watching a crew wait for the copy to be typed for the scene we are about to film.

3705 Production Unit

Here we assume that we are not shooting on film at all, but are using videotape. This practice is becoming prevalent, and I suspect that within the foreseeable future film also will appear only in museums and videotape will replace it entirely. By that time, I will have revamped this budget to reflect that change.

Most of the time we will hire a videotape production firm to handle the whole package for us, and we will go through the bidding process with them. This actually is where you will become familiar with videotape, rather than reading this brief section.

3706 Video Display

Description	Amount	Units	X	Rate	Subtotal	
Prep	0	Day	1	500	0	
Shoot	0	Day	1	500	0	
Wrap	0	Day	1	500	0	
Personal Equipment Rental	0	Day	1	0	0	
Car Allowance	0	Day	1	0	0	
	0		1	0	0	
Package Rental	0		1	0	0	
Monitors	0		1	0	0	
Playback Units	0		1	0	0	
Cassettes/Supplies	0		1	0	0	
Transfers: Film-Tape	0		1	0	0	
Delivery/Shipping	0		1	0	0	
Misc Charges	0		1	0	0	
Total					**0**	

Supercarrier had numerous scenes that called for computer read-outs, radar monitors, and the like. We were lucky to have Jay Heit, a genius who delivered exactly what the scene required within our ridiculously short pre-production times, on videocassettes that could be cued properly and timed to camera.

Once again this usually will be a package rental situation, and we will probably pay for the machinery and operator in one fee.

Even if we have subcontracted out the video production, we may still have to purchase the videotape itself.

3707 Video Rawstock

Description	Amount	Units	X	Rate	Subtotal	
1" Video Masters	0		1	0	0	
3/4" Video Masters	0		1	0	0	
Protection 1/2" Video	0		1	0	0	
Color Correction	0		1	0	0	
Time Coding	0		1	0	0	
Total					**0**	

I hesitate to catalogue the many videotape formats available at this time. We can change this account to suit. When I started working in Videotape at CBS in 1963 we used 2-inch tape that I had to edit with scissors, Freon, and a magnifying glass. Now, with modern technology, I understand that Freon causes holes in the ozone layer over Antarctica and the scissors have been replaced by electronic editing machines.

3800   Studio Facilities

Acct#	Account Title	Page	Total
3801	Rehearsal Stages	51	0
3802	Shooting Stages	52	0
3803	Back Lot/Ranch	52	0
3804	Electric Power	52	21,819
3805	Heating/Air Conditioning	52	0
3806	Studio Charges	52	0
3807	Office Charges	52	0
3808	Construction Charges	53	0
3809	Storage Space	53	0
3810	Dressing Rooms	54	0
3897	Loss & Damages	54	0
3898	Miscellaneous	54	0
3899	**Total Fringes**		**3,350**
	Total		**25,169**

Movie Magic Budgeting - [BUDBOOK.MMB ~ 3800 ~ Studio Facilities]
BUDBOOK.MMB   2,671,976   Cume: 0
Category 3800   25,169   Change: 0

In general, the studio will try to get as much money as possible while providing a minimum of service, and it is our job to give it as little money as we can while getting a maximum of service. We must watch out for hidden costs or costs not bargained for before we film. And we must be especially careful that our use and rental of absolutely every facility at the studio is carefully spelled out in the rental agreement.

A Catch-22 is built into almost all studio rental deals and we are well advised to be wary of it. Most studios not only rent stage space but also insist that we rent its equipment package and use its commissary, first-aid facility, security system, and dressing rooms. If we are filming, say, for six weeks and are in studio only during week 4, what are we going to do about our own equipment rental package, motor homes, caterer, and so forth, for that week? We have hired our own equipment and caterer based on a six-week shoot. Suddenly, in the middle lies a week during which we can't use our own equipment. What will happen to the equipment? Will we return it to the rental house for the week, and if so, when the week is over will we get back the same equipment? Do we pay for two sets of equipment for that week?

One obvious answer is to plan all our studio filming for the last week of the film, and rent our own package only for the first five weeks. Much of the time our schedule can accommodate such a circumstance. But, in case it cannot, we must be prepared beforehand to bargain with both the equipment rental house and the studio to make the best possible deal.

3801 Rehearsal Stage

Description	Amount	Units	X	Rate	Subtotal
Setup	0		1	0	0
Furniture	0		1	0	0
Rental	0		1	0	0
Misc. Equipment	0		1	0	0
Floor Tape	0		1	0	0
Total					**0**

During pre-production on many shows that are very heavy in the personal relationship area, the Director may wish to rehearse the talent prior to filming. It is helpful to have the Art Director lay out on the rehearsal stage floor, the floor plans of the major sets to be used during the film and also to have a smattering of tables and chairs, nothing fancy, mind you, but enough to sit on. A large table for readings and discussions of character also is advisable. The table usually will have some soft drinks and snacks on it as well.

3802 Shooting Stage

Description	Amount	Units	X	Rate	Subtotal
Construction	0		1	0	0
Hold	0		1	0	0
Shoot	0		1	0	0
Wrap	0		1	0	0
Restore	0		1	0	0
Total					**0**

I have rented shooting stages in the oddest places. Most of the major studios in Los Angeles now have rental stages, and we can rent the bare four walls with no crew. In most cases, an equipment rental package comes with the studio and we will be forced to take it, as mentioned already. When we rent the studio's equipment, we may have to carry on our payroll a studio employee whose purpose is to make sure that we don't use the equipment in ways not intended by the manufacturer. For example, the employee may object if we use three-wire cable to haul our trucks out of the mud during a rainstorm. (I actually saw a crew do this once!)

Restore

Many studios require that when we are finished filming we have to repaint the studio back to where it was prior to our being there. One studio always insists that the shooting company remove nails from the walls, remove the set pieces, and so on., not an unreasonable request.

3803 Backlot

Few backlots are left from old Hollywood and fewer ranches. Fox Ranch has been converted to a county park. Parts of Paramount Ranch are being developed as a suburb. Warner Ranch has long since become Woodland Hills. Columbia Ranch still exists as a small patch of nostalgia in the East San Fernando Valley. Universal still has all its property, which we can see by going on the Universal Tour.

I remember filming on the Universal back lot. I had to call the tour office two days in advance to tell them when I would be filming so that it could schedule a detour around our shooting company. What is actually interesting is the large numbers of industry executives who got their start in the biz by driving those Universal Studios Tour trams.

Backlots are paid for in the same manner as any other studio facility, and the same care must be taken in forming the rental agreements.

3804 Electric Power

MMB	Movie Magic Budgeting - [BUDBOOK.MMB -- 3804 -- Electric Power]					_ ₽ ×

MMB	File Edit Setup Tools Library Go To Magic Window Help					_ ₽ ×

BUDBOOK.MMB	2,671,976	TOP SHEET		Cume:	0
Category 3800	25,169	ACCOUNT		Change:	0
Account 3804	21,819	DETAIL			

Description	Amount	Units	X	Rate	Subtotal	▲
Generator Time Charges	0		1	0	0	
Local 40 Man	0		1	0	0	
Overtime allowance	10	%	1	0	0	
Shoot	4	Weeks	1	1,784.30	7,137	
Shoot Distant	6	DistWks	1	2,447.04	14,682	
Total					**21,819**	

Whatever studio we rent will supply us with all the power we might need as long as we pay for it. We probably will pay for either the power or the Generator Operator or both, or an equitable combination. We also will have to pay for the Operator's overtime on the in the unlikely case that we film after 5:30 PM. We may be able to work out a deal whereby we share the cost of the Operator with other movie companies on the same lot. Each studio works differently in this regard. Some studios, which are converted warehouses, such as some in Valencia, provide no power at all and we may have to bring in our own generator.

3805 Heating and Air Conditioning

I have rented studios in the past that were not air conditioned. I also have rented studios that were converted warehouses, in which the air conditioning system was not silent. The system then had to be tied into the Sound Mixer's panel so the Mixer could turn it off and on for takes.

Incidentally, it is essential that the makeup area be cooled. A hot Actor will sweat and it is twice as hard to makeup someone who was sweating.

3806 Studio Charges

Description	Amount	Units	X	Rate	Subtotal
First Aid	0		1	0	0
Security	0		1	0	0
Mill	0		1	0	0
Phones	0		1	0	0
Phone Operators	0		1	0	0
Commissary	0		1	0	0
Commissary Overtime	0		1	0	0
Electric/Grip Package	0	Week	1	0	0
Parking	0		1	0	0
Dressing Rooms	0		1	0	0
Studio Overhead	0		1	0	0
Cleanup/Restore	0		1	0	0
Total					**0**

(Screen header: Movie Magic Budgeting - [BUDBOOK.MMB - 3806 - Studio Charges]; File Edit Setup Tools Library Go To Magic Window Help; BUDBOOK MMB 2,671,976; Category 3800 25,169; Account 3806 0; Cume: 0; Change: 0)

Some studios charge us for personnel to watch over their material when we rent it. We will have to hire a studio electrician as our best boy to make sure that we do not massacre the studio's cables or barn doors. This probably will be in addition to our own best boy, because, being of kind heart, we will not wish to lay off that person for the few days we will be in studio.

First Aid Department

We may find to our dismay that even though we have a company Medical Attendant, the studio has charged us for the use of its dispensary to stay open while filming was taking place.

Security Department

While on a major lot we will be under the watchful eye of the studio security system. More than likely the studio will insist that we use their security personnel and will not allow us to bring our own onto the lot. As long as we let them know where our work is, they can guard our material (within reason), detour tourist busses around us, and help us with parking, among other things. The point is that we will not need to have our own security folk.

We must be sure that all this is spelled out in our studio facilities rental agreement. We might be assuming that our security is taken care of when it is not.

The Mill
Most studio facilities have a "mill." It usually has a complete set of the machine tools used in set construction, as well as a volume discount on wood and other materials we will be using. It usually is well worth considering using studio facilities for the ease of operation, rather than farming out the construction to an outside firm, which will build our sets elsewhere, dismantle them, transport them to the studio, and remantle them on the stage.

<u>Mill</u>: A building used for construction.

Telephone and Telex
We will use the studio switchboard if we are on a major lot, and each studio has its own idiosyncratic phone system. Usually, these systems include an operator whose overtime we will have to pay if we shoot past a certain hour.

Commissary
Most studio commissaries have better than average food. The chefs and waiters understand the need for speed as well as good, solid food for a working crew.

Parking
We have to be sure that there is sufficient parking for our crew. Some studios have lots that charge a parking fee. Some of the warehouse-turned-studios have insufficient parking nearby and we might have to hire a minivan just to shuttle the crew from an adequate parking lot to the stage and back.

3807 Office Charges
Most of the items such as Auditors, Art Department, Construction, and so forth, under the Office Charges account, refer to the studio employees for whom we might be billed at the end of filming. Once again, be sure that the studio facilities rental agreement spells out everything we may be using from the studio, to avoid unpleasant surprises.

3809 Storage Space Rentals
Never assume that we will have the space to put unused flats against a wall of a studio we rented. This is entirely illegal, because all the fire control laws require a walking space right next to the walls of a studio. Therefore, we always need space to store the unused sets, props, and the like during filming. We also may want to save some of the material for our next show, and it will have to be stored somewhere other than in an expensive studio facility.

If we have built a particular set and storage is a problem, we may try to sell it to another producer making a film with similar needs. We can recoup a little construction money that way. It is even a savings if we just give it away, as long as the new owner pays for all the cartage and cleanup. Then at least we don't have to clean up the studio, saving us money in the process.

3810 Dressing Rooms

Description	Amount	Units	X	Rate	Subtotal
Portable	0		1	0	0
Motor Homes	0		1	0	0
Dressing Room Building	0		1	0	0
Total					**0**

Most major studios have portable dressing rooms that they will rent for a pittance. Some are worth about that, being little wooden boxes like 7-foot-cube packing crates; others are more plush. Many have no air conditioning or heating and must be so supplied.

To make matters worse, some studios will not allow us to bring a honeywagon or star dressing rooms on the lot, insisting that we rent their rooms. Be sure to know what the rooms look like before any rental agreement is signed.

The business of personal dressing rooms was started many years ago with William Randolph Hearst, who was ever watchful of the comfort of his special friend, Marion Davies. Hearst got her a very luxurious trailer for a dressing room, which was hauled from stage to stage so Miss Davies could relax between takes. After that, it took all of about five minutes for other stars to see the advantage of having their own trailers parked near the stage, and now a proper trailer has become something of a status symbol for actors.

3900 Atmosphere

Acct#	Account Title	Page	Total
3901	General Extras	54	0
3902	Stand-ins	54	0
3903	Silent Bits	54	0
3904	Special Ability	54	0
3905	Minors	54	0
3906	Welfare Workers/Teachers	54	0
3907	Dancers/Singers	54	0
3908	Sideline Musicians	54	0
3909	Interviews	54	0
3910	Wardrobe Fittings	54	0
3911	Wardrobe Allowance	55	0
3912	Misc. Rentals	55	0
3913	Extras Casting	55	0
3914	Crowd Controllers	55	0
3915	Payroll Service	55	0
3997	Loss & Damage	55	0
3998	Miscellaneous	55	0
3999	**Total Fringes**		**0**
	Total		**0**

Atmosphere, Background Talent, Extra Talent – all these terms refer to the folks who perform in the film but have no written lines. These are the crowds in crowd scenes, the other couple at a dinner for four, when only the two principals have speaking lines, and so forth. They earn their pay by being present and by blending into the background. There are exceptions, but the rule is that an Extra is an Actor who has no written lines and is not directed by the director.

3901 General Extras
The majority of extras are General Extras. These stalwarts add flesh to a scene without being obtrusive.

3902 Stand-Ins
A Stand-in is a person of about the same height, build and coloring as a principal Actor. While a set is being lit, the D.P. needs a body to stand in the Actor's position on the set. The Actor himself usually is in makeup, rehearsing, or otherwise occupied. So the D.P. has this person to stand in for the Actor; hence, Stand-in. Stand-ins, being present every day, eventually become part of the crew. They usually make a tad more money than a regular extra. At times, an Actor will request a particular Stand-in. It is wise to accede to the request because, generally, the stand-in knows where the Actor is when we don't.

3903 Silent Bits
A Silent Bit takes place when an Extra acts or reacts with a principal character, such as the desk clerk at a hotel who checks in the Actor, without dialogue. As long as the character is silent, he or she can be an Extra. We pay a premium for silent bits, and the Extras doing them will be worth it.

3904 Special Ability
We used to call this a *horse*, because back in the old days, horseback-riding extras received a premium payment for their special ability. Any special ability that adds to a scene usually is worth something extra. A bartender who knows how to shake a good drink, a skateboarder, an ice-skater, or rollerblader – all these should be paid for their ability. I have a friend who is a court stenographer. Whenever I have to film a scene in a courtroom, I hire this fellow to sit in front of the judge's bench and act like a court stenographer. He brings his stenotype machine and takes down all the dialogue. I've even seen directors ask him to read back some lines as spoken because it's faster than winding back the tape to listen to it.

Special ability fees are extra money paid on top of basic Extra's rate, much like stunt adjustments.

3905 Minors
Remember that a minor is still a minor if only an Extra, and still must have Welfare Teachers and the like and state law for study time and play time must be strictly observed.

3909 Interviews
We may need to interview Extras for particular situations. On the TV series *Supercarrier* we needed military types with military haircuts to play the naval officers on the show. We had the Extras casting folk send in several dozen people who were willing to have their hair cut in regulation military length, and we chose the best two dozen or so. They became the stock company for the show. We probably will have to pay a pittance for an interview to the interviewees.

3910 Wardrobe Fittings
After we cast the Extras for *Supercarrier* we had to have them custom-fitted with naval uniforms. We had to pay for their time for that also; not much, but it was worth it.

3911 Wardrobe Allowance
On *War and Remembrance* we filmed full-dress evening dances with Army, Navy, and Army Air Corps officers and their ladies, and the scenes took place in 1943-1944. By golly, Cenex, the Extras Casting people, managed to pull together 600 people who came to the set in period clothes to be in the show. We paid them extra for the use of their special period wardrobe. Many of the ladies showed up in 1940's hairstyles as well, saving us even more time.

3912   Miscellaneous Rentals

Description	Amount	Units	X	Rate	Subtotal
Automobiles	0	Days	1	30	0
Trailers	0	Days	1	19	0
Skates, Skateboards	0	Days	1	5.50	0
Bicycle	0	Days	1	12	0
Golf clubs & Bag	0	Days	1	12	0
Moped	0	Days	1	15	0
Motorcycle	0	Days	1	35	0
Police Motorcycle	0	Days	1	50	0
Pet	0	Days	1	23	0
Camera or luggage (per piece)	0	Days	1	5.50	0
Tennis Racquet	0	Days	1	5.50	0
Skis (Incl Boots & Poles)	0	Days	1	12	0
Binoculars	0	Days	1	5.50	0
Large portable radio	0	Days	1	5.50	0
Total					**0**

An Extra who is asked to bring his or her own car and drive it in a shot must be paid for the use of the car in the picture. Even more if it is a special model of car, such as an old "Woodie" station wagon or a Ferrari Testarossa, although I know many more Extras who own Woodies than who own Ferraris. The Screen Actors Guild has mandated prices for the rental of personal property for use in the film.

3913   Extras Casting

More than likely we will use one of the excellent casting services to cast our Extras for us. Casting our own Extras is a very unusual move. The Extras Casting company must have a vast database of people from which to choose.

When on location in a major city there we will probably find someone well versed in gathering large numbers of Extras for the film. The local Film Commission will help us with that. In not-so-large population centers, it may be wise to contact local theatre groups, Theatre Arts Departments of local colleges, and so forth.

Generally speaking, Extras Casting people will charge us around 9 percent of the total cost of the Extras for the casting service and another 6 percent or so to handle the Extras payroll. This can be a great time and money saver if we have many Extras. The service will supply us with complete details of the hours each Extra worked, adjustments for special business, and so forth along with the bill for each week.

Of course the A.D.s are well versed not only in directing background talent but also in handing out the adjustments at the end of each day.

3914 Crowd Controllers

If there are many extras, for example, during a crowd scene for the inauguration of an Egyptian Pharaoh, it may be helpful to hire people who are accustomed to handling large numbers of extras and their vouchers swiftly and efficiently. It could save us time and money to have people like that around in some cases. They usually will be paid as extras, but at a slightly higher daily rate.

Extras Voucher: Form an Extra fills out to enable the company to pay him or her properly. It includes the hours worked and notations for any adjustments. If an Extra claims that an adjustment is due and the A.D. decides against it, that too is noted. Eventually SAG will become involved if the adjustment was really deserved.

4000 Production Film and Lab

Acct#	Account Title	Page	Total
4001	Production Raw Stock	55	117,600
4002	Production Develop	55	55,717
4003	Print	55	73,037
4004	Sound	56	0
4005	Projection	56	0
4006	Videocassettes	56	0
4007	Video Format Transfers	56	0
4099	**Total Fringes**		**0**
	Total		**246,354**

The prices in this account change with astonishing frequency. They also vary depending on our needs, the amount of film being purchasing or processed, and so forth. Film price changes are announced regularly in the trade papers, and we should follow them closely rather than take this book as gospel. Things can shift that fast. As for processing costs, I have paid both major labs and minor labs varying rates and have had good and bad experiences with both. I remember one major lab, no longer in business, that toward the end of its existence assigned a representative to stay on its clients' sets to commiserate whenever some idiot in the lab dropped the film into the bath by accident. I also have had very small independent labs service me without a hitch. So it's your choice. As a very broad rule, larger, more established labs have a much wider range of services and perform them better than smaller labs.

This account deals with whatever we will need for the production period only, which is to say, only our raw stock costs, developing, printing, and dailies. Everything else will be accounted for in the post-production area. Even so there may be variations, as it is becoming more and more prevalent for a company to shoot on film, develop the negative, and then print the negative directly to videotape or digitize the print to a magnetic medium like magneto-optical drives, with reference numbers, edit the tape or files, do the entire post-production process on tape, then conform the negative for prints later. More about this in the post-production area.

4001 Production Film

Description	Amount	Units	X	Rate	Subtotal
1st Unit Normal Negative	280,000	Feet	1	0.42	117,600
1st Unit Hi-speed	0	Foot	1	0.46	0
Extra Cameras Normal	0	Foot	1	0.42	0
Extra Cameras Hi-Speed	0	Foot	1	0.46	0
2nd Unit Normal	0	Foot	1	0.42	0
2nd Unit Hi-Speed	0	Foot	1	0.46	0
Special Visual FX	0	Foot	1	0.46	0
Total					**117,600**

(Window info: BUDBOOK.MMB 2,671,976 / Category 4000 246,354 / Account 4001 117,600. Cume: 0 Change: 0)

Obviously some film stocks have not been figured in here, and many others have not yet been invented. Just add them as they occur. Eastman Kodak is still the standard, but we may wish to use Fuji stock, or Agfa, or Ilford. All are perfectly good film stocks, each with its own pleasures and pains, and whichever our D.P. wants is what the company should provide. I also have not provided for 16mm film in here, as it is so seldom used on features. (However, I must mention that a recent TV show I filmed was on 16mm.) Just remember, if we use 16mm, we may not be able to project our film in major theaters with as much success as with 35mm or 70mm. The grain will be pretty fierce.

The rule of thumb is this: budget 5,000 feet of 35mm film for each camera per day. As we are filming for 56 days on our theoretical schedule, the program has automatically calculated 280,000 feet of film.

4002 Production Developing

Description	Amount	Units	X	Rate	Subtotal
1st Unit Develop	280,000	Feet	0.9	0.2211	55,717
Extra Cameras	0	Foot	1	0.2211	0
2nd Unit	0	Foot	1	0.2211	0
Spl. Visual FX	0	Foot	1	0.2211	0
Force Develop 1 Stop	0	Foot	1	0.2837	0
Force Develop 2 Stops	0	Foot	1	0.313	0
Total					**55,717**

(Window info: BUDBOOK.MMB 2,671,976 / Category 4000 246,354 / Account 4002 55,717. Cume: 0 Change: 0)

The figures given here came from the latest price list from CFI, one of the industry's premier laboratories. I always estimate that I will be developing 90 percent of what we shoot, hence the 0.9 in the x column.

4003 Print

Description	Amount	Units	X	Rate	Subtotal
1st Unit	280,000	Feet	0.65	0.4013	73,037
2nd Unit	0	Foot	1	0.4013	0
Total					**73,037**

As mentioned previously, more and more production companies are shooting on Negative stock, developing, and transferring directly to tape or digital media for editing.

Digital editing always is faster and more facile than editing on film with a Moviola or flatbed. Videotape and computer systems, such as Avid or D-Vision, enable us to preview a cut before actually making it. Cutting and splicing film does not permit this. So, even though film editing is less expensive because of the equipment rental, the overall costs can be equivalent because of the speed and facility with which computer and videotape systems may be used.

We discuss this entire area more thoroughly in the post-production sections of the book.

4100 Tests

Acct#	Account Title	Page	Total
4101	Screen Tests	56	0
4102	Makeup Tests	56	0
4103	Wardrobe Tests	56	0
4104	Camera Tests	56	0
4199	Total Fringes		0
	Total		0

4101 Screen Tests

These are not often done any more, but there will always be shows in which a particular role requires the knowledge of how a person will appear on screen. In days of yore there were several producers who promised screen tests to young aspiring actresses in the hope of some physical favor in return. It was not unknown for those producers to keep one of their crews after shooting, bring in the actress, and have a screen test shot of her, ensuring the producer's social activity of the evening. Usually in such cases there was no film in the camera and it was all a charade for the starlet's benefit, or lack thereof, as the case may be.

You might have used Account 1610 for screen tests, in which case this account should be ignored to avoid duplication. Some Producers wish to have a separate account for tests, some wish to include tests in the Talent category.

4102 Makeup Tests

If we need a special makeup for a horror sequence, burns, or some other special effect, it is always wise to see how the final product will appear on film.

4104 Camera Tests

Sometimes a D.P. has not used, say, Fuji film before, and will wish to run exposure tests on it, see what its latitude is, stuff like that. Or the D.P. may not have used the new Panavision Einsteinium Package and wants to put it through its paces. This account is where those tests should be charged.

4200 Second Unit

Acct#	Account Title	Page	Total	
4201	Crew	56	0	
4202	Equipment	56	0	
4203	Locations	56	0	
4204	Transportation	57	0	
4205	Film/Lab	57	0	
4299	**Total Fringes**		**0**	
	Total		**0**	

(BUDBOOK.MMB   2,671,976   Category 4200   0   Cume: 0   Change: 0)

The Second Unit is a separate production unit intended to photograph stunts, effects, and other shots requiring the presence of neither the Director nor cast nor sound. Only stunt doubles and photo doubles are filmed in a second unit. The first unit Director is not present, being occupied with the First Unit. In fact the second unit is almost always shooting at the same time as the first unit, to help out with time or logistic problems. If the First Unit Director or cast is present, or if dialogue is recorded, it becomes a First Unit and the presence of a larger production crew becomes necessary.

Second units always are filmed simultaneously with the First Unit. For instance, after I have finished filming on a street location and have wrapped the crew to move to the next location, I might leave a Second Unit at the first location to photograph some car drive-bys and stunts. This would happen while the First Unit is in the process of moving or even shooting the first few shots at the next location.

Second Units can be shot after the first unit has completed principal photography. I generally suggest that Second Unit be formed after the Editor has made an assembly of the shots. This way we will know exactly what added shots are necessary. Then we can hire a Second Unit Company or Stock Footage Firm for all the missing establishing shots, run-bys, and so on.

Usually we make a package deal with Second Unit Companies or Stock Shot Firms, in which we pay them a package rate per day's work, or per foot of film, or some variation. In case we have to put together our own Second Unit the Detail account attached will prod our memory for people and things we may need.

Post-Production

Up to now we have been dealing only with the production, or shooting, area of the budget. Equally important to the final form of the film will be the editing process, which includes additional entities such as music and opticals, not to mention the possible addition of computer graphics.

Post-production begins the minute the film leaves the camera at the end of the first day of filming. At that point the film is taken to the laboratory for processing, and the next day (we hope) the Director and Editor will view the "dailies" together and discuss how the scenes will be edited. This process is collaborative. The Director must supply the Editor with enough film to enable a scene to be edited properly, and the Editor must cut that film to carry out the wishes of the Director in giving the scene its greatest psychological impact.

So, in post-production, all the ancillary devices that contribute so much to the movie are added in, all those things which we can't find on the set. Music, sound effects, visual effects, all the manipulation of sight and sound that cannot happen on the set in real time happen here.

5100 Editing

Acct#	Account Title	Page	Total
5101	Post Prod'n Supervisor	58	0
5102	Editor	58	48,000
5103	Assistant Editor	58	37,298
5104	Extra Editors	58	48,000
5105	Extra Assistants	58	48,000
5106	Apprentice Editor	58	27,452
5107	Music Editor	58	0
5108	Sound FX Editor	58	0
5109	ADR Editor	58	0
5110	Supplemental Assistants	58	0
5111	Extra Apprentices	58	27,452
5112	Secretaries	59	0
5113	Editing Rooms/Rentals	59	0
5114	Editing Supplies	59	0
5115	Storage	59	0
5116	Coding	59	0
5117	Projection	59	0
5118	Continuity	59	0
5119	Librarian	59	0
5120	Videocassettes	59	0

Editing is the one element which separates Film and Video from all other art forms. In no other art can one destroy linear time and rebuild it in psychological terms. A moment can be twice as long to one person as it is to another. To a girl waiting for her boyfriend to return from a trip, a five-minute wait at the airport can be like five hours. The two-hour trip home, after he has arrived can be like five minutes. Through the editing process the Editor can extend or compress time to suit the feelings of the people involved.

The editing process has changed radically in just the last few years. As more and more younger editors move into the workplace, the methods of editing evolve. Even the veterans are using the computer systems these days. Avid and D-Vision are widely used in editing rooms around the world, and Moviolas and flatbeds are quickly being consigned to the scrap heap. Most editors who have worked with digital editing systems see no reason ever to edit film again.

5101 Post-Production Supervisor

Movie Magic Budgeting - [BUDBOOK.MMB — 5101 — Post Prod'n Supervisor]						_ ᴮ X
File Edit Setup Tools Library Go To Magic Window Help						_ ᴮ X
BUDBOOK.MMB 2,671,976			TOP SHEET ACCOUNT DETAIL		Cume: 0	
Category 5100 305,934					Change: 0	
Account 5101 0						

	Description	Amount	Units	X	Rate	Subtotal	▲
▸	Prep	0	Weeks	1	1,500	0	
▸	Shoot	0	Weeks	1	1,500	0	
▸	Post Production Local	0	Week	1	1,500	0	
	Personal Equipment Rental	0	Weeks	1	0	0	
	Car Allowance	0	Week	1	0	0	
	Total					**0**	

This function is interchangeable with "Associate Producer" in the classic sense. Unless we have an extremely intricate editing problem, the Editor can handle the entire post-production process for us (with proper monetary consideration). Sometimes the Producer will do it. However, when a number of post-production elements complicate the situation, such as post-production video effects, traveling mattes, multiple effects, and music tracks that have to be coordinated, the presence of a supervisor to handle the details may be necessary.

As a rule the post-production chief, whatever the title, will start working on the first day of production, because the lab work, synching dailies, and sometimes even assembly begins on that day.

In a TV series, it is almost always necessary to have a Post-production Supervisor or Associate Producer because three or four shows will be edited at once. Someone will have to coordinate the ADR, music, opticals, and so on for all the shows, and the most efficient way to do this is to have the entire post-production situation funneled through one office. We may be looping people from three different shows on a single day, or Foleying for two separate shows, and someone has to organize it all.

5102 Editors

Movie Magic Budgeting - [BUDBOOK.MMB — 5102 — Editor]						_ ᴮ X
File Edit Setup Tools Library Go To Magic Window Help						_ ᴮ X
BUDBOOK.MMB 2,671,976			TOP SHEET ACCOUNT DETAIL		Cume: 0	
Category 5100 305,934					Change: 0	
Account 5102 48,000						

	Description	Amount	Units	X	Rate	Subtotal	▲
•▸	Shoot	4	Weeks	1	2,000	8,000	
•▸	Post Production Local	20	Weeks	1	2,000	40,000	
						48,000	
	Overtime allowance	10	%	1	0	0	
▸	Travel	0	Day	1	0	0	
	Total					**48,000**	

The Editor makes the picture what it is. I often think that all of us, – Director, Actors, Producers, D.P.s, – all of us exist only to create little strips of celluloid to give to the Editor, with which to work magic. It is his or her job to re-create an action in its psychological time and disregard its physical time. The text that follows will discuss the different editing systems currently in use.

Editors seldom have any prep time. They almost always start work on the first day of filming and continue through many weeks of post-production after the filming has finished. But we can't forget that an Editor who must be on distant location will be paid for travel time.

5103 Assistant Editor

The Assistant Editor is an immensely important cog in the editing machinery. On a recent show I produced, the Editor was entirely unfamiliar with electronic editing and a little resentful that we were editing on tape and not film. We were lucky to have an Assistant Editor available who was knowledgeable and personable and who taught the Editor all about the new system. Within two weeks, the Editor was comfortable with the system and now will use nothing else. The Assistant became invaluable by keeping the logs properly and keeping the cassette machines loaded properly, and was so good at his job that we raised his title to Associate Editor. Unhappily we could not raise his salary as well, but at least he got some prestige.

Assistant Editors these days function as computer experts, handling data entry and logging as much as in the old days they kept the little snippets of film from getting mixed up. The details of keeping the Editor supplied with the elements necessary have changed over the last two or three years. Now it's computer stuff, like magneto-optical drives and bernoullis.

5104 Extra Editors

I have worked under conditions in which we finished filming a movie of the week and had to deliver it two weeks later. That's when we usually hire an editing team under one master Editor, who then supervises editors who work simultaneously on other parts of the show.

5106 Apprentice Editors

Editing is a very difficult task. It is absolutely essential that new editors be trained constantly to enter the ever-widening business. Apprentices can not only learn a useful and artistic means of livelihood, but also learn which Editor drinks coffee without sugar.

5107 Music Editor

A Music Editor works with the Music Composer in front of a Moviola, flatbed, or digital editing system, editing the music to fit the picture. This person is usually present during scoring sessions, and is an integral part of the music team. This is discussed further in the Music Account, 5400.

5108 Sound Effects Editor

A Sound Effects Editor has to create an aural picture to supplement the visual one. I remember a scene in which a young boy slept peacefully in a house on the beach. Suddenly in the mix we heard a loud fog horn on the FX track. The sound editor thought it was appropriate, neglecting the fact that it would have awakened the sleeping child.

5109 ADR or Looping Editor

The ADR Editor must edit the dialogue tracks recorded in the ADR sessions so that they match with the lip movements of the Actors.

5113 Editing rooms/Rentals

We begin the editing process when we begin production. We must have an Editor on staff when we begin filming to have our dailies "synched." Even if we are editing electronically the Editor must coordinate the process.

More important, the Editor will begin the assembly during production. The Editor will be arranging the shots in the order the scenes suggest, and, when dailies are viewed, will consult with the Director as to how the scenes should be cut.

For this reason we need an editing room and supplies, whether it be for film or electronic editing systems.

5116 Coding

This process is done electronically if we are editing electronically. If we are editing film, coding is done by imprinting the film itself with the code number with a mechanical ink stamper.

5117 Projection

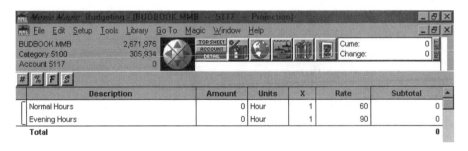

Pre-Production

If we have made screen tests or makeup or wardrobe tests, or if we are viewing other shows for potential talent of one kind or another, we need to screen the results somehow.

Dailies – Executives and Crew

We need projection sessions of dailies for both the crew and executives, especially if a large hierarchy back at the studio must see dailies. If we are shooting a TV movie or series, the Network will screen the dailies for itself.

Film and Video Transfer

Sometimes, instead of seeing dailies in the regular way, in a screening room, the Director and D.P. will ask for VHS video cassettes to view at home. This is not as good a system as seeing the dailies full-frame in a screening room and should be used only if no screening facilities are available. On videocassette there is no chance of catching a slightly out-of-focus shot, or seeing a mike shadow if one appears at the edge of frame. It always is preferable to see the dailies on a big screen on film.

Location Theater

When filming on distant location in a small town somewhere in the Midwest, I have rented a local movie theater and shown dailies after the regular show lets out. One time while I was filming in the Bahamas, the theater refused to stay open past its closing time but did interrupt the normal movie to show our dailies. The audiences in the theater, for the week we were there, were treated to our dailies during the course of their regular show – in the middle of the movie, yet! And the viewers didn't even notice that anything was different from the movie they were watching.

I also have rented a screening trailer more than once, a trailer fitted out by an enterprising projectionist with a small double-system projection room and a screening room with everything built in.

Note: Be sure that the Theater you rent for dailies has double-system sound. you will need a sound dummy to play your track. Otherwise you will be watching silent dailies!

> **Double system**: Picture and sound are on separate rolls of film.
> **Sound dummy**: Tape player which cannot record.

5122 Travel and Living

Sometimes when on distant location for an extended period of time we will want the Editor along. The film will be processed in Hollywood and shipped back to location where the Editor syncs the dailies and views them with us.

It also is becoming more common for dailies to be digitized and sent via T-1 phone lines across the country. This means that the Editor no longer must be in the same room as the Director and Producer, or even in the same city. More and more companies are filming in Toronto, sending the film to a lab, and having the dailies digitized and put online, then projected through the T-1 line to the Director in Toronto, the Editor in Hollywood, and the Producer at his home office in Palm Springs. All three can watch the dailies at the same time and discuss them in real time on the phone while the dailies show on their computer screen courtesy of the Internet. They even can run a take back and forth if they wish, just as in a real projection room, to discuss a particular line and how it's spoken.

5200   Post-Production Film and Lab

Acct#	Account Title	Page	Total
5201	Reprints	60	0
5202	Color Master Positive	60	17,558
5203	Duplicate Negatives	60	17,558
5204	Develop Optical Negative	60	921
5205	Negative Cutting	61	5,850
5206	Answer Prints	61	14,474
5207	Release Prints	61	0
5208	Stock Footage	62	0
5298	Miscellaneous	62	0
5299	**Total Fringes**		**1,449**
	Total		**57,810**

I was lucky in that Jim Nelson, who produced the post-production on such cinematic monuments as *Star Wars*, helped to design the post-production section of this budget. Like most production persons, until recently I was much more knowledgeable about the production end of pictures than about the post-production end.

A new development has appeared in film processing lately. More and more labs are offering electronic processing services. A leader in this field at the moment is Laser-Pacific which offers what it calls an *Electronic Lab*. It can take the undeveloped negative, process it, transfer it directly from a negative to whichever electronic medium we prefer, and provide editing rooms for Avid, D-Vision, or some other process.

5201   Reprints

Description	Amount	Units	X	Rate	Subtotal
Editor's Reprints	0	Foot	1	0.4013	0
Timed Color Reprints	0	Foot	1	0.7466	0
Print"B" Negative	0	Foot	1	0.4013	0
Total					**0**

The Editor starts by editing the work print, which is usually a one-light print struck by the lab off the original negative. If the Editor is editing on film, using a Moviola or flatbed of some kind, eventually the film will become more and more dirty, or the perfs will shred, and reprints will be needed. Editing on a digital machine does not require reprints because everything will be available on electronic media. More reprints will be necessary for the Music and Sound Effects Editors.

5202 Color Master Positive

Description	Amount	Units	X	Rate	Subtotal
After first trial incl. wetgate - A roll	9,000	Feet	1	1.9509	17,558
Without first trial - A roll	0	Feet	1	3.4734	0
Individual scenes for opticals	0	Feet	1	3.0013	0
Each add'l roll	0	Feet	1	0.1559	0
Composer's Video Xfer	0	Allow	1	100	0
Video Cassettes	0	Roll	1	10	0
Color Reversal Dupes	0	Foot	1	0	0
Total					**17,558**

BUDBOOK.MMB 2,671,976
Category 5200 57,810
Account 5202 17,558
Cume: 0
Change: 0

After the film is completely edited, but before the music and effects tracks are added, the negative itself is cut to the exact length of the finished film. Then a Color Master Positive is printed off the negative, and the original negative is sent to the vault.

Notice that our entry of 9,000 feet has been automatically inserted to calculate the cost of the Color Master Positive, properly multiplied out for us to CFI's rate.

5203 Duplicate Negatives

Description	Amount	Units	X	Rate	Subtotal
Complete reels from interpositive	9,000	Feet	1	1.9509	17,558
For FX and extra scenes	0	Feet	1	3.0013	0
Total					**17,558**

BUDBOOK.MMB 2,671,976
Category 5200 57,810
Account 5203 17,558
Cume: 0
Change: 0

When we have finished all the processes of color correction and timing, we will be ready to use the Color Master Positive to strike a number of Dupe (duplicate) Negatives. These will be used to make the Release Prints.

5204 Develop Optical Negative

Description	Amount	Units	X	Rate	Subtotal
Tests	0	Foot	1	0.1023	0
1st Final Dubb (Mono)	9,000	Feet	1	0.1023	921
1st Final Dubb (Stereo)	0	Foot	1	0	0
Post-Preview Dubb (Mono)	0	Foot	1	0.1023	0
Post-Prev. Dubb (Stereo)	0	Foot	1	0	0
Foreign Dubb (Mono)	0	Foot	1	0.1023	0
Foreign Dubb (Stereo)	0	Foot	1	0	0
TV Version Dubb	0	Foot	1	0.1023	0
35/32mm (For 16mm Prints)	0		1	0	0
Total					**921**

(BUDBOOK.MMB 2,671,976 / Category 5200 57,810 / Account 5204 921 / Cume: 0 / Change: 0)

Dialogue used to be recorded on magnetic tape during production. The tape was then transferred to film in the form of an optical sound track for editing, Since the advent of electronic editing systems, this is seldom done, but eventually we will have to develop and print an optical track for making our "married" or single-system prints, in which the picture and sound are put together on one piece of film for projection in theaters.

Although many theatres in large urban areas have CD capability, and THX, most theatres in more rural areas have no such systems and still must rely on the old standard, an optical sound track. So every movie still has an optical sound track, and if all else fails, the projectionist can shift quickly to that.

5205 Negative Cutting

Whether we have edited our show on videotape or film, we have to go back to the negative, cut it to conform to the final length of the film, shot for shot, and strike our Color Master Positive prints. Then we will carefully store the negative in a vault.

The negative is irreplaceable. We take out "negative insurance" because anything that happens to our movie usually is reflected in this piece of irreplaceable film.

Safety Film

In early days, until about 1949, all 35mm film was shot on nitrate base film, called *cellulose nitrate*, chemically closely related to TNT. Nitrate film is extremely volatile and spontaneously combustible. It will catch on fire faster than most Fourth of July fireworks. And it explodes if enough of it catches fire at once. If it doesn't explode, it will deteriorate slowly, over years, and while it does so, it emits a colorless, tasteless, odorless gas which is lethal. This is not a good thing to keep around the house, although quite a few old-timers from the movie industry have kept some old nitrate stock and given it to their children without explaining the hazards of the stuff. If you know such a person he or she should be warned. The fire department generally will dispose of it for you, or the HazMat people. But keeping it is a very bad idea indeed.

Since 1949 it has been illegal to film with nitrate film. At that time cellulose acetate became dimensionally stable enough to photograph professional films, and it is the standard now. Acetate-based film still is known as "safety film."

5206   Answer Prints

Description	Amount	Units	X	Rate	Subtotal
Silent Answer Print	0	Foot	1	1.6082	0
1st Answer Print (Mono)	9,000	Feet	1	1.6082	14,474
1st Ans. Print (Stereo)	0	Foot	1	1.6082	0
Post-Prev. Ans. Prt	0	Foot	1	0	0
Foreign Ans. Print	0	Foot	1	0	0
TV Version Ans. Print	0	Foot	1	0	0
Unsqueeze/Scanning	0	Foot	1	0	0
16mm Answer Print	0	Foot	1	0	0
70mm Blowup Print	0	Foot	1	0	0
Stripe 70mm Print	0	Foot	1	0	0
Xfer Sound to Print	0	Foot	1	0	0
Xfer Video to Film	0	Foot	1	0	0
Color Timing Charge	0	Foot	1	0	0
1st Answer print	0	Foot	1	0	0
Total					**14,474**

BUDBOOK.MMB 2,671,976
Category 5200 57,810
Account 5206 14,474

Cume: 0
Change: 0

An answer print is struck after all the color-correcting and other chemical manipulating has been completed in the lab. The print includes the sound track, as it would be in a theatre; hence it provides the "answer" to the question of whether the film is projectable. There may be several answer prints, each better than the last, until a perfectly acceptable one is finally delivered.

Unsqueezing and Scanning

This refers to converting feature films for viewing on television. Feature films are photographed almost always in the aspect ratio of 1.85:1, whereas TV still emulates the old academy aperture of 1.33:1. This leaves an area at either side of the screen that will not appear on TV. An electronic scanning system is used that pans across the larger feature film frame to focus on the relevant action and put it on the TV screen, when it may not have appeared by normal transfer without scanning.

Aspect ratio: The ratio of the width to the height of the image. Normally the "Academy Aperture" is 1.33:1, or 4:3. That's about what TV is as well. CinemaScope is 1.85:1. And the old VistaVision was 2.15:1.

Unsqueezing refers to the old CinemaScope system with an anamorphic lens, which squeezed the extrawide image onto regular 35mm film. Another anamorphic lens was necessary during the projection process to unsqueeze the image, or else everyone on screen looked a great deal thinner than normal, like the people in a Modigliani painting.

5207   Release Prints

Description	Amount	Units	X	Rate	Subtotal
35mm Release Prints	0	Foot	1	0.4025	0
Foreign Version Prints	0	Foot	1	0.4025	0
TV Version Prints	0	Foot	1	0.4025	0
Sub-Titled Prints	0	Foot	1	0.4025	0
16mm Prints	0	Foot	1	0.7045	0
Videocassettes	0	Roll	1	10	0
Xfer film to VC	0	Hour	1	333	0
Master Positive	0	Foot	1	1.6274	0
Dupe Internegative	0	Foot	1	1.6274	0
Separation Masters	0	Foot	1	1.6274	0
Printing Masters	0	Foot	1	1.6274	0
16mm Reduction Negative	0	Foot	1	1.3779	0
Total					**0**

BUDBOOK.MMB 2,671,976 / Category 5200 57,810 / Account 5207 0 / Cume: 0 / Change: 0

Release Prints usually are paid for by the Distributor. The Producer is responsible for everything up to and including the Answer Print; after that the Distributor bears the brunt of the lab costs.

Take note that several different kinds of release prints are available for different purposes. If a Distributor will be releasing prints overseas, the prints must be dubbed into the native languages, or at least subtitled. For the TV version some of the more colorful language may have to be removed, as well as some of the more libidinous or violent scenes.

5208 Stock Shots

Description	Amount	Units	X	Rate	Subtotal
Viewing Prints	0	Foot	1	0.5732	0
Interpositives	0	Foot	1	2.8913	0
Dupe Negatives	0	Foot	1	2.4991	0
Stock Shot License Fee	0	Foot	1	30	0
Reels	0	Foot	1	11.33	0
Shipping Cases	0	Foot	1	23.02	0
Messenger to Neg. Cutter	0	Foot	1	100	0
Coding Negative	0	Roll	1	17	0
Film Cleaning	0	Roll	1	23	0
Film Storage	0	Foot	1	0	0
Total					**0**

We always assume that we will need stock footage. There is always the odd establishing shot of the hospital or courthouse we didn't have time to shoot. Companies, such as Carl Barth's Stock House, not only have large libraries of stock shots but also will shoot our building for us and sell us the film as if it were stock footage, at great savings.

We have to bear in mind that the acquisition of stock footage involves several steps. First we have to view what is available and select the footage we need. Then we have to rent the negative from the stock footage house, have the film printed onto stock like the one we're using, give the footage to the editor to cut into the film, have a dupe negative made for the negative cutter to insert into the original negative, and finally include the shots in the release prints. Most stock footage is kept on videocassette today, so the viewing part is easier than it was.

5300 Post-Production Sound

Acct#	Account Title	Page	Total	
5301	Music Scoring Stage	62	0	
5302	Music Dubb-Down Stage	62	0	
5303	ADR Stage	62	0	
5304	Foley Stage	62	0	
5305	Sound Effects	62	0	
5306	Temp Dubbs	62	0	
5307	Rehearse Stage	62	0	
5308	Pre-Dubb	63	0	
5309	1st Combine Dubb	63	0	
5310	Post-Preview Dubb	63	0	
5311	Foreign Dubb	63	0	
5312	TV Version Dubb	63	0	
5313	Recorders	63	0	
5314	Dolby	63	0	
5315	Other Sound Royalties	63	0	
5316	Dubbing Supervisor	63	0	
5317	Dubbing Equipment Rental	63	0	
5318	Mag Stock & Transfers	63	0	
5319	Optical Sound Transfers	63	0	
5398	Miscellaneous	63	0	

This is the period in which the sound is made rational. The human ear hears sounds selectively, and these sounds are filtered further by the brain into the relevant and irrelevant categories. A studio microphone has no such ability, so the post-production sound folk must do it for us. Stray sounds always creep into our track while we are filming; now we can equalize them out. We also can add interesting new sounds to give the picture more life.

We will need several sound tracks and have to mix them together to make a single sound track that flows evenly with the visuals. The major areas we will concentrate on are music, sound effects, and dialogue. The dialogue track is what we have recorded on location while the actors were speaking the lines. Sometimes the dialogue track will be the ADR track because we had to rerecord the dialogue (see Account 5303).

5301 Music Scoring Stage

Description	Amount	Units	X	Rate	Subtotal
Pre-Score	0	Hour	1	550	0
Post-Prod. Scoring	0	Hour	1	650	0
Stage Set-up Charges	0		1	400	0
Special Equipment	0		1	300	0
Total					**0**

In real life no bands follow us around. In the movies, music appears suddenly from out of nowhere. As Mayor Shinn said in *The Music Man*, "Where's the band?" Here, on the scoring stage. With the conductor (usually also the composer) standing there with earphones, staring at a large screen and conducting the band in time to the editing. Please see Account 5400.

5303 ADR Stage

Description	Amount	Units	X	Rate	Subtotal
ADR Stage	0	Hour	1	400	0
Narration Stage	0	Hour	1	250	0
Total					**0**

ADR (automatic dialogue replacement, or "looping") is necessary when a live recorded sound track is unusable for some reason. The actors come to the sound studio. They watch the original scene projected on a screen and listen through earphones to their original lines, then try to reproduce their lines to match their lip movements on the screen. Because they are seeing the same bit of film over and over again on a loop, this is called looping.

We probably can use the same studio in which we recorded the ADR for our narration track if necessary.

5304   Foley Stage

Description	Amount	Units	X	Rate	Subtotal	
Stage	0	Day	1	310	0	
Record Wild Sound FX	0	Day	1	250	0	
Foley Walkers	0	Day	1	350	0	
Walla Crew	0	Day	1	750	0	
Props Purchased/Rented	0		1	0	0	
Total					**0**	

(Window title bar: Movie Magic Budgeting - [BUDBOOK.MMB - 5304 - Foley Stage])
(Menu: File Edit Setup Tools Library Go To Magic Window Help)
(BUDBOOK.MMB 2,671,976 Category 5300 0 Account 5304 0   Cume: 0 Change: 0)

Foley: the process of creating live sounds for the sound effects track.

Record Wild SFX

At times it might be necessary for us to send a Sound Recordist into the swamp to record the mating cry of the Louisiana alligator or some other unique but vital sound. I once had a producer who insisted on using the cries of the humpback whale in a soundtrack. No, I didn't send out a Recordist in a scuba suit to make the recording; we found a CD with the sounds already recorded.

Foley Walkers

The people who actually create the sounds are called Foley Walkers. Foley Walkers have developed the art to a fine pitch by now, and the craft is exacting. They will have several wood trays on the floor, bearing different kinds of walking surfaces, such as gravel, tile, grass, sand, rocks, and parquet. As the scene calls for it they record their footfalls in coordination with the picture. They also may make sounds of bodies falling, people hitting or slapping each other, chains clanking, swords rattling, and whatever else may be necessary for the sound track.

Walla Crew

Walla crew is what we call the people who make the miscellaneous vocal sounds for crowd scenes. In the old days it consisted of a bunch of people standing around a microphone and saying, "walla-walla-walla-walla" in different tones of voice. When we do the same thing with extras on set, it is called *Omnies*. We used to ask the Extras to stand around and say, "omnie-omnie-omnie-omnie-omnie" into the microphone for crowd scenes.

Prop Purchase and Rental

This comes under the heading, "things that make interesting noises." The use of coconuts to reproduce hoofbeats is an example. We will need chains and other pieces of metal, bells, and other objects that make sounds.

5305 Sound Effects

Description	Amount	Units	X	Rate	Subtotal
Rights	0		1	0	0
Rerecording	0		1	0	0
Stock	0		1	0	0
Total					**0**

Many capable sound effects houses in Los Angeles will be willing to handle our sound effects package. Most sound effects are on CD today. The sound effects company will read the script and collect the appropriate sound effects for our show. Then we give the company a cassette of the film, and the company matches the sound effects to the film, shot for shot. What we get for our money is a sound track with only the sound effects on it, called the *effects track*.

5308 Pre-Dubb

Description	Amount	Units	X	Rate	Subtotal
Dialogue	0	Hour	1	550	0
FX	0	Hour	1	650	0
Music	0	Hour	1	550	0
Total					**0**

Also called the *pre-mix*. Now, we have several tracks in our hands, covering three areas: the Effects Track, the Music Track, and the Dialogue Track. And we might have several versions of each for different purposes. For instance, for the dialogue track we might have one recorded on location and one recorded in ADR. We might have several FX tracks, one for crowd noises, one for car engine noises.

In the pre-mix we carefully line up these tracks in the mixing machine opposite the video which each matches. This is a time-consuming process but absolutely essential for the mix itself. The mix can cost up to twice as much as the pre-mix so we don't want to waste mixing time lining up the tracks.

5309   First Combine Dubb

Description	Amount	Units	X	Rate	Subtotal	
Mono	0	Hour	1	750	0	
Stereo	0	Hour	1	800	0	
Total					**0**	

Also known as *the mix*. All the tracks have been lined up during the pre-mix, and now we have a huge mixing console in front of us. Sitting in a big room with a wide screen in front of us, we project the movie, stopping at each frame, deciding how the sound is to be designed for each shot. For some shots we lower the volume on the music and turn up the effects. For heavy dialogue pieces, we may lower the music and effects and turn up the dialogue. We might have a drive-by shot of the cars chasing down the street. So we turn down the dialogue track and turn up the sound effects of the cars motors, recorded on location, and the extra effects track of the tires squealing on the pavement. That's what mixing is, blending together all the tracks into a cohesive whole, concentrating on the appropriate sound for the current shot.

We end up with two tracks: the mixed track with everything on it, and the M & E track with only the music and effects without the dialogue. We have to provide this last track to the foreign distributor, who will use our M & E track and record a dialogue track in the native languages of the foreign countries where the picture will be shown. Then these will be combined in a special native language track, for each country.

5311   Foreign Dubbs

Our picture probably will become so outstandingly successful that distributors from all over the world will approach us for the right to distribute in their home countries. They must hire a cast of polyglots to re-record the entire dialogue track using foreign translations of the original words. These translations must be carefully designed so that even though the words are foreign they match the lip movements of the cast as closely as possible. The cost of this process usually is borne by the foreign distributor.

5312   TV Version Dubb

This replaces some of the more obscure scatological and sexual references in our script with words acceptable to Network Standards and Practices. Words such as "Gee Whiz" and "Golly" replace the more offensive street vernacular.

5314 Dolby

The Dolby system has become de rigueur for the movie business. We don't like the hiss we hear on our car tape deck? Just imagine what it would sound like in 70mm stereo quadraphonic with 250 watts of power in a screening room!

When we use the Dolby system, we will be required to contribute an patent royalty of several thousand dollars to the Dolby organization, thereby guaranteeing good sound for our movie.

5400 Music

Acct#	Account Title	Page	Total
5401	Composer	64	0
5402	Lyricist	64	0
5403	Music Coordinator	64	0
5404	Arrangers/Orchestrators	64	0
5405	Conductor	64	0
5406	Copyists/Proofreaders	64	0
5407	Musicians	64	0
5408	Singers	64	0
5409	Rehearsal Pianist	64	0
5410	Music Coaches	64	0
5411	Sound-Alikes	64	0
5412	Recording Facilities	64	0
5413	Music Stage Labor	64	0
5414	Rights/Royalties	64	0
5415	Re-recording	64	0
5416	Music Package Fee	64	0
5498	Miscellaneous	64	0
5499	**Total Fringes**		**0**
	Total		**0**

Music for movies is a very intricate and delicate matter. It must be a part of a whole, supplementing the visuals, yet not so obtrusive as to call attention to itself. In the best of all possible worlds one can find a music score that also is able to sell records of itself.

There are two ways to make music for a movie. We can have it composed especially for the show and record it or we can buy existing music and lay it in. The former usually is more expensive but far more satisfying and more to the point. Making something work is never as good as creating something from scratch to work for you.

The Composer has had the cassette of the edited work print since the day after it was finished and has been composing the music to fit the visuals, shot by shot. Then the Music Producer will hire an orchestra, or whatever size of band is required, book the studio with microphones and recording equipment, projector and screen, and set up the recording session. On large pictures, the music track might take days to record, much like recording a regular music CD.

On the other hand, pictures like *American Graffiti* used pre-recorded music exclusively to brilliant effect, but that is the exception rather than the rule.

5411 Sound-Alikes

Sometimes we would like a particular vocal group to sing one of its hit songs for the soundtrack, but we lack the money. So we buy the rights from the Music Publisher to rerecord the music and we hire a sound-alike group to do the singing. After all, who's gonna know?

5416 Music Producer

In many cases it will be advantageous to hire a Music Producer to handle the entire music package. This is a financial arrangement, not an aesthetic one, much like jobbing out the construction costs to an independent contractor for building the sets. We still have complete control of the music, only we have hired a company to handle the project instead of hiring each Musician individually and we paid for the studio ourselves. We pay one bill for all the music and the Music Producer becomes the employer of record for the musicians. We hand the Music Producer a check and receive the music track.

5500 Titles

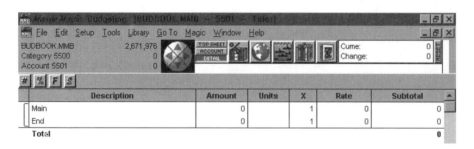

Acct#	Account Title	Page	Total
5501	Titles	65	0
5502	Creative Design	65	0
5503	Background Photography	65	0
5504	Film/Lab	65	0
5505	Travel/Lodging	65	0
5506	Title Package Fee	65	0
5507	Subtitles	65	0
5598	Miscellaneous	65	0
5599	**Total Fringes**		**0**
	Total		**0**

There are many kinds of titles. The simplest are the kind shown on my Dad's old home movies, chalk letters on a blackboard photographed straight on without any frills. During the 1930s and 1940s it was common for dramas to have the titles shown in the form of a gloved hand turning pages in a guest book or calling cards falling onto a silver tray.

Our titles will be affected by our budget, of course. The more money we have to spend the more elaborate the titles can be. Companies specialize in title design and execution, so we can subcontract this just like the music.

5501 Titles

Description	Amount	Units	X	Rate	Subtotal
Main	0		1	0	0
End	0		1	0	0
Total					**0**

When I first got into the biz, it was common for all the titles to be at the front of the picture, and highly unusual for there to be any credits at all at the end. Nowadays, it is common for the credits to be almost as long as the picture itself, but at least they are at the end of the show so that viewers can leave the theater or remove the cassette from the VCR and not have to watch lists of names meaningful only to the respective next of kin.

5502 Creative Design

Description	Amount	Units	X	Rate	Subtotal
Design Fee	0		1	0	0
Special Art Work	0		1	0	0
Title Setting/Layout	0		1	0	0
Photography	0		1	0	0
Total					**0**

The creation of titles has become an art in itself. The titles for the *James Bond* films, for instance, immediately and forcibly sets the tone of the movie to come. The end credits for *Around the World In 80 Days*, the original Mike Todd production, brilliantly recap the picture in their reminder to the audience of which actors appeared in cameos in which scenes.

5503 Background Photography

Description	Amount	Units	X	Rate	Subtotal
Cameraman: Local	0		1	0	0
Cameraman: Distant	0		1	0	0
Assistant	0		1	0	0
Other Labor	0		1	0	0
Equipment Rental	0		1	0	0
Materials/Supplies	0		1	0	0
Misc. Photography Charges	0		1	0	0
Total					**0**

This section is used only if a special Cameraman has been hired only to photograph the background scenery for our titles. This is also termed *Process Plates*. A Cameraman has been provided in the Camera department as well.

5504 Film/Lab

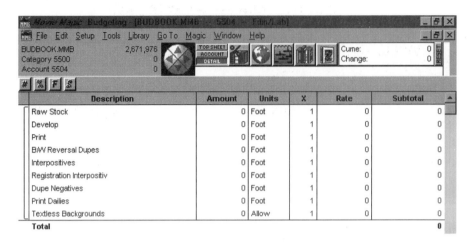

Naturally, because we will be filming titles, we need to have the film developed, printed, and eventually edited into the final prints.

5506 Title Package Fee

We use this account only if jobbing out the title package to a subcontractor.

5600 Optical Effects

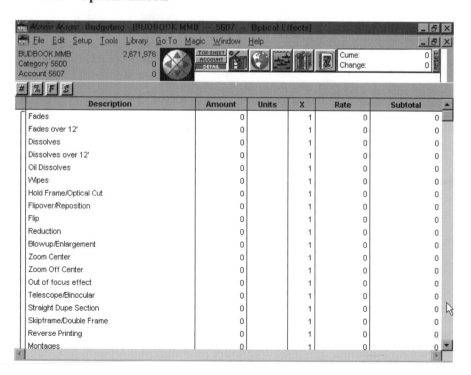

5607 Optical Effects

Acct#	Account Title	Page	Total
5601	Supervisor	65	0
5602	Coordinator	65	0
5603	Assistant Coordinator	66	0
5604	Consultants	66	0
5605	Special Editorial Labor	66	0
5606	Other Labor	66	0
5607	Optical Effects	66	0
5608	Matte Department	66	0
5609	Process Plates	67	0
5610	Animation	67	0
5611	Inserts	67	0
5612	Raw Stock	67	0
5613	Laboratory	67	0
5614	Travel/Lodging	68	0
5698	Miscellaneous	68	0
5699	**Total Fringes**		**0**
	Total		**0**

Description	Amount	Units	X	Rate	Subtotal
Fades	0		1	0	0
Fades over 12'	0		1	0	0
Dissolves	0		1	0	0
Dissolves over 12'	0		1	0	0
Oil Dissolves	0		1	0	0
Wipes	0		1	0	0
Hold Frame/Optical Cut	0		1	0	0
Flipover/Reposition	0		1	0	0
Flip	0		1	0	0
Reduction	0		1	0	0
Blowup/Enlargement	0		1	0	0
Zoom Center	0		1	0	0
Zoom Off Center	0		1	0	0
Out of focus effect	0		1	0	0
Telescope/Binocular	0		1	0	0
Straight Dupe Section	0		1	0	0
Skipframe/Double Frame	0		1	0	0
Reverse Printing	0		1	0	0
Montages	0		1	0	0

Remember how Billy Bitzer invented the iris by accident on a D.W. Griffith film? He closed down the iris before he stopped turning the crank. Opticals have grown some since then.

Nowadays it is almost as common for opticals to be created by computer as it used to be to have pages fly off a calendar to denote passage of time. Computers are very facile instruments, capable of creating all sorts of special effects impossible to do by any other means.   More and more computer animation is being used to wonderful purpose not only in movie titles but also in TV commercials.

Optical effects can be as expensive as we want to make them. They should be used whenever photographing the real event is physically impossible, as in *Star Wars*, or when using actors in a real situation can put their lives in jeopardy, as in Spielberg's *Indiana Jones* series. The prices will vary according to the magnificence of our vision.

Most of these opticals are self-describing, and most can be accomplished in our digital editing machine so we can see exactly what they will look like on the screen. We won't be imparting the opticals to the original film per se, but we will be noting that "This wipe goes here" in the EDL (edit decision list), which the computer generates for the negative cutter and the lab to indicate their use of the original negative.

5608   Matte Shots

Description	Amount	Units	X	Rate	Subtotal
Supervisor	0		1	0	0
Matte Painters	0		1	0	0
Assistants	0		1	0	0
Matte Cameraman	0		1	0	0
Assistant Cameraman	0		1	0	0
Space rental	0		1	0	0
Camera/Stand Rental	0		1	0	0
Painter Supplies	0		1	0	0
Camera Supplies	0		1	0	0
Matte shots contracted	0		1	0	0
Misc. Matte Dept. Charges	0		1	0	0
Total					**0**

Norman Dawn was a cameraman from the silent era. He developed the "Glass Matte" into an art form. If a mountain did not exist he would paint it on a piece of glass and photograph the scene through the glass, aligning the mountain as if it were there. The mountain appeared on the screen just as if it were actually there. His book was a source of wonderment and joy to me as a child.

Matte: When something is superimposed over the picture of something else to add to a scene an element not otherwise present.

5609   Process Plates

Description	Amount	Units	X	Rate	Subtotal
Plates Cameraman, Local	0		1	0	0
Cameraman, Distant	0		1	0	0
Assistant, Local	0		1	0	0
Assistant, Distant	0		1	0	0
Camera Rentals	0		1	0	0
Camera Supplies	0		1	0	0
Total					**0**

Process, *Plates*, *R.P.*, *Rear Projection* are all terms which refer to essentially the same process. Finding it difficult to transport the cast and crew to Ulaanbaatar, Mongolia, for two shots? The simple solution is to send a Cameraman there to take a few shots of typical streets or views of the nearby River Orhon. Back in Hollywood, set up a large screen in a studio. On one side of the screen, set up a very bright projector in which is threaded the Mongolian footage. On the other side of the screen, set up the camera and actors. Run the projector and camera on Selsyn Synch motors so they will stay in synch. Turn on both simultaneously. Now the actors will play out their scene in front of a projected scene of Mongolian streets, and the audience will believe that our actors actually were there.

This system works quite well for Front Projection as well, but we have to beware of shadows on the screen. For that matter, we have to beware of the same with Rear Projection.

This category just as well could have been included in the production part of this budget, because rear projection plates are generally filmed during principal photography.

5614   Travel and Lodging

Description	Amount	Units	X	Rate	Subtotal
Travel	0		1	0	0
Lodging	0		1	0	0
Per Diem	0		1	0	0
Car Rental	0		1	0	0
Total					**0**

In 1968 I did a movie for Columbia called *Pendulum* filmed on location in Washington, DC, when Martin Luther King Jr., was assassinated. Washington was in flames, mobs were running through the streets, and filming was obviously impossible. We packed up the whole company and sent everyone back to Hollywood. I returned to my home in New York. Three weeks later, I took a Cameraman back down to Washington to film some background plates for the film, the scenes were shot with Rear Projection, and no one was the wiser. Of course, if you see the movie now on late-night TV you will see through the rear window of Jean Seberg's cab some smoke rising from buildings in the background. This account covered our travel and lodging expenses.

5700 Post-Production Video

Acct#	Account Title	Page	Total
5701	Off-Line Editing	68	0
5702	On-Line Editing	68	0
5703	Additional Equipment	68	0
5704	Additional Services	69	0
5705	Studios/Rooms	69	0
5706	Transfer & Assembly	69	0
5707	Laydown from Master	69	0
5708	Layback to Video Master	69	0
5709	Layback to Videocassette	69	0
5710	Audiotape Rental	70	0
5711	Audiotape Purchase	70	0
5712	Videotape Purchase	70	0
5713	Pre-Blacking/Time Coding	70	0
5714	Travel/Lodging	70	0
5798	Miscellaneous	71	0
5799	**Total Fringes**		**0**
	Total		**0**

As time progresses it is becoming more and more prevalent to edit digitally. My last six or so shows have been photographed on film. The negative was developed, transferred to electronic media, and everything after that, including delivery to the network, was done on computer. If we are working on a theatrical film, we can edit digitally, then conform the negative to the edit decision list and strike prints from it. If we are working on a television film it is even simpler. The negative need never be touched again. Edit on tape, release on NTSC. If we need a PAL or SECAM print, that can be transferred from our NTSC print very simply.

NTSC: (**N**ational **T**elevision **S**ystem **C**ommittee) 525 scan lines, 30 frames per second. Standard for North America, Japan, some other countries. Also known as **N**ever **T**wice the **S**ame Color.

PAL: (**P**hase **A**lternation **L**ine) 625 scan lines, 25 frames per second. Standard in most countries of Western Europe and some other countries throughout the world. Also known as **P**eace **A**t **L**ast.

PAL-N: a variation of PAL, having a different color subcarrier frequency for broadcast. Used only in Argentina, Paraguay, and Uruguay. These countries accept standard PAL recordings.

PAL-M: Brazilian version of PAL. 525 Lines, 30 frames per second. PAL-M and PAL are not interchangeable without conversion. Also known as **P**ay **A** **L**ittle **M**ore.

SECAM: (**S**équence **C**ouleur **A**' **M**émoire) 625 scan lines, 25 frames per second. The French standard, also adopted by Eastern Europe, Russia, parts of the Middle East. Also known as **S**omething **E**ssentially **C**ontrary to **A**merican **M**ethods.

SECAM utilizes two different types of color sync encoding. Depending on the country, it may be either SECAM V (Vertical), used in France and Russia, or SECAM H, (Horizontal), common in the Middle East. Today most 2-inch, 1-inch and ¾-inch SECAM recordings are made with both V and H encoding for color playback in any SECAM country.

½-inch SECAM VHS equipment does not allow simultaneous V and H encoding. VHS SECAM V recordings will play back on SECAM H equipment. But only in black and white – and vice versa. Thuis, when ordering VHS SECAM conversions or copies, V or H encoding must be specified to assure a proper color playback.

The above descriptions were supplied by Michael Papadaki, my personal post-production guru and Exec. VP of Sales for Consolidated Film Industries (CFI).

As we can see from the plethora of formats, a variety of editing methods certainly is available to the enterprising producer.

5701   Off-Line Editing

Description	Amount	Units	X	Rate	Subtotal	
Editor	0	Day	1	0	0	
Assistant Editor	0	Day	1	0	0	
Facility	0		1	0	0	
Equipment	0		1	0	0	
Xfer Film: 2" or 1"	0		1	0	0	
Xfer Film: 3/4" or 1/2"	0		1	0	0	
30 Min. 3/4" VC	0		1	0	0	
30 Min. 1/2" VC	0		1	0	0	
Xfer Tape-Tape (Cutting)	0		1	0	0	
VC 60 Min 3/4"	0		1	0	0	
VC 60 Min 1/2"	0		1	0	0	
Misc. Supplies/Cassettes	0		1	0	0	
Clean List	0		1	0	0	
Conform Film from Tape	0		1	0	0	
Total					**0**	

Off-line editing generally refers to the time when the editor and assistant sit in the editing room with an Avid system or the equivalent, working alone without the advantages of an entire digital system.

5702 On-Line Editing

Description	Amount	Units	X	Rate	Subtotal	
2-VTR Editing	0		1	0	0	
3-VTR Editing	0		1	0	0	
4-VTR Editing	0		1	0	0	
5-VTR Editing	0		1	0	0	
3/4" - 1" Mastering	0		1	0	0	
3/4" - 3/4" Mastering	0		1	0	0	
Set-up Charges	0		1	0	0	
Total					**0**	

In on-line editing. the usual process, the Editor sits in a control booth with a Video Operator, going back and forth with the original Video Master, conforming it to the "work print," which had been done on the off-line editing system.

> **Work Print**: The film or tape which we actually edit, or work on.

5705 Studios/Rooms

Description	Amount	Units	X	Rate	Subtotal	
Sweetening Room	0		1	0	0	
Prelay Room	0		1	0	0	
Spotting Room	0		1	0	0	
Screen Room	0		1	0	0	
3/4" or 1/2" Viewing Room	0		1	0	0	
1" or 2" Viewing Room	0		1	0	0	
Total					**0**	

Sweetening Room
I always liked the expression *sweetening* as applied to post-production sound. It sort of reminds one of maple sugar in Vermont in the fall. In the movies, it refers to making the sound track better.

Prelay Room
Here we do a preliminary sound mix, lining up all the elements, music, dialogue, and effects, for the mixdown. Prelay is the equivalent of the Pre-Dubb, and the Mixdown is equivalent to the Mix.

> **Mixdown**: The process by which we combine the sound elements onto a single soundtrack.

Spotting Room
Here, the picture is projected on a screen, and the Producer, the Editor, and the Music Composer decide at which points or "spots" the music is to appear.

Screening Room
Here is where we screen the work print at various stages. *Screening* usually refers to film projection, whereas

5706 Transfer and Assembly

Description	Amount	Units	X	Rate	Subtotal
VT to Audiotape	0		1	0	0
Audiotape to VT	0		1	0	0
Interstandards Transfer	0		1	0	0
Pin-Stripe SMPTE Code	0		1	0	0
Multitrack to Multitrack	0		1	0	0
Nagra Transfers	0		1	0	0
Assembly Time	0		1	0	0
Total					**0**

(Movie Magic Budgeting — [BUDBOOK.MMB — 5706 — Transfer & Assembly]. File Edit Setup Tools Library Go To Magic Window Help. BUDBOOK.MMB 2,671,976. Category 5700 0. Account 5706 0. Cume: 0 Change: 0.)

Interstandards Transfer
This is our NTSC-to-PAL or -SECAM transfer for foreign release. Several good videotape houses in Los Angeles can accomplish this in such a way that nobody would ever know the difference between the original and the transfer.

Nagra Transfers
Nagra transfers are sound transfers for videotape. The Nagra portable recorder has been the standard for live sound recording for years in the movie business. When I started in the biz, we used Westrex trucks and 35mm tape. The trucks were parked outside the sound stage or just off camera on location. They were insulated so that the microphones could not hear the tape recorders humming. Since air conditioning had not yet been made portable enough, the Sound Recordists sweated a lot.

Nagra: A brand of professional audiotape recorder manufactured to very exacting specifications in Switzerland.

5710 Rental/Purchase of Audiotape
It is impossible right now to tell where the science and art of audio recording is going. The advent of Digital Audio Tape already has affected the market, and recordable compact disks are coming into widespread use. Regular audiotape, which has held sway over the recording industry for lo these many years, is already becoming obsolete.

5800 Facilities

We have allowed an entire account for facilities. We never know when we will need it. We may be working with a major studio on its lot and have to provide for a facilities fee in our budget to cover the studio overhead. This is where that goes.

Other Charges

This finishes the post-production section of our budget. There are a few budget areas which require acknowledgement, but which don't fall neatly into any of the previous categories. These still need detailed examination and must be addressed on a line-item basis.

6100 Insurance

Acct#	Account Title	Page	Total
6101	Pre-production Cast	72	0
6102	Cast	72	0
6103	Negative & Video	72	0
6104	Faulty Stock	72	0
6105	Errors & Omissions	72	0
6106	Props/Sets/Etc.	72	0
6107	3rd Party Liability	72	0
6108	Guild Accident & Travel	72	0
6109	Other Misc. Insurance	72	0
6110	Medical Examination Fees	72	0
6111	Miscellaneous	72	0
6199	**Total Fringes**		**0**
	Total		**0**

I read a science fiction short story that took place about 100 years into the future. Insurance companies had taken over the world. There were no longer any police or armies, only adjustors.

The cost of insurance has just exploded in cost over the last few years. For expendience, I usually apply a percentage amount of the budget for insurance rather than trying to estimate each insurance figure individually – 1.75 percent is an adequate fee. This will vary, of course, depending on the difficulty of our show and how many stunts and effects are in the script. The insurance company will insist on reading the script prior to shooting to be able to estimate the insurance premium.

When we buy insurance we almost always exclude the cost of the script and post-production from the budget figure under which we will estimate the above 1.75 percent. After all, the script already is purchased and needs no insurance. And the post-production takes place in the editing room, where the Editor, one hopes, cannot use the Avid to run down any passers-by on the sidewalk.

6101 Pre-Production
We probably will buy some insurance during pre-production, for instance, because if any DGA member is flying our DGA contract provides for flight insurance, and we will want to take out a blanket policy to cover eventualities.

6102 Cast Insurance
Cast insurance protects the production against losses incurred due to the sickness or death of an actor. Generally one has the five main Actors and the Director insured against anything untoward happening during filming. Knock wood, I have never had to make a claim on this kind of insurance at all.

We could run into a situation as I did on a show a few years back. Some scenes were being filmed in New York with two Actors from Los Angeles. The insurance company informed us that one Actor had had a heart attack recently and was uninsured for flying. What to do? Send The Actor four days early by train? Nope, we figured the risks and he flew to New York and back in fine fettle. His heart attack had nothing to do with flying.

6104 Faulty Stock: Insurance
We may run into a bad batch of film and expose it before we know that it is flawed. The chances of this are almost nil, but it has happened. We should be insured for that.

> **Stock**: The medium on which we are recording the images, such as film or tape.

6105 Errors and Omissions
We are not perfect and make errors and omissions, so this category is often essential. We probably will use this category quite a bit. It covers, among other things, clearances.

Many years ago I shot a documentary in New York about slum lords. We photographed a building downtown that was as good a slum as any. We had cleared the building legally with the owner and the city. The establishing shot, however, included a small piece of a corner of the building next door. Wouldn't you know? The owner of the building next door sued the TV station for invasion of privacy, libel, and a lot of other unpleasantness and came away several thousand dollars richer.

We must also be very careful that the names of our characters have been checked. If we are filming a true-life story we may find that a person whom we have named in the script will sue us for using that person's real name and likeness without permission. While our Errors & Omissions insurance covers this it is always better to avoid the problem in the first place.

6106 Props, Sets, and the Like
We may have some loss or damage on sets, props, or wardrobe. Typically we will have a deductible of $2500 in this category, so we must be careful.

6107 Third Party Liability
A movie was being filmed outside a bank several years back. The scene called for some robbers to exit the bank carrying their assault weapons. The Producer had decided to take advantage of passing traffic as free extras, so he instructed the Police not to hold up traffic for the shot. A driver saw the "robbers," panicked, and hit the accelerator instead of the car brakes. The car jumped the curb and struck quite a few passers-by before coming to rest

against a lamp post. Whom did the passers-by sue? Not the driver. They sued the Producer. Most accidents, when they happen, are not quite this extreme in their results. Also, the Producer usually is less culpable than this one. But we have to be covered for all emergencies.

6108 Guild Accident and Travel

Screen Actors Guild and DGA, among other unions, require Producers to carry flight insurance and hazardous duty insurance. We like to think of ourselves as being completely safe, but miscellaneous crew members have walked into airplane propellers while preoccupied with the next shot.

6109 Other Miscellaneous Insurance

Description	Amount	Units	X	Rate	Subtotal
Fixed Wing Aircraft	0		1	0	0
Helicopter	0		1	0	0
Watercraft	0		1	0	0
Total					**0**

Our show may call for flights by fixed wing aircraft, rotary-wing aircraft, Hovercraft, underwater devices – who knows? Better safe than sorry. Let the insurance agency know what is going on so that we can be covered for any possibility.

6110 Medical Exams

Any Actor who is to be insured must be examined first. Some doctors in Los Angeles specialize in movie exams. Some will even come to the studio to save us time. This is a nice thing to remember when we are about to start filming.

6200　Legal Costs

We can put this in as an allowance here. Theatrical law is a highly specialized practice and most attorneys are unable to handle it without having spent some time apprenticing at a theatrical law firm. All contracts and other legal situations must be checked with these people. Show biz is the world's biggest target and we can come to grief if we don't cover ourselves legally.

Truth be told, we have fostered this attitude ourselves. Publicity is aimed at convincing everyone how successful and rich we are when the truth is usually somewhat less than that. But the public perception of show biz is that everyone is a millionaire and can afford to pay thousands of dollars on frivolous lawsuits. So a good attorney is essential.

Not to have an attorney handle the talent contracts is asking for trouble. Actors have attorneys making the contracts, and we Producers have to be protected as well.

When I budget a project I usually assign 1.5 percent of the total direct costs for legal fees.

6300   Publicity

Acct#	Account Title	Page	Total
6301	Publicist	72	5,981
6302	Assistant Publicist	72	9,219
6303	Secretary	73	5,600
6304	Stillsman	73	0
6305	Graphic Artist	73	0
6306	Other Labor	73	0
6307	Public Relations Fee	73	0
6308	Design Work	73	0
6309	Trade Paper Ads	73	0
6310	Press Screening Charges	73	0
6311	Special Still Photography	74	0
6312	Publicity Office Expenses	74	0
6313	Entertainment	74	0
6314	Travel & Lodging	74	0
6398	Miscellaneous	74	0
6399	**Total Fringes**		**7,057**
	Total		**27,857**

Our business thrives on publicity. No business in the world goes so far out of its way to get a mention in newspapers or on TV news – and rightly so. The more people hear about a show, the more they will want to see it; and that's where our income is. It is not unusual for movie distribution companies to spend somewhere near the actual production cost of a film to publicize it. The returns make it all worthwhile. This is a business, after all. Economically, if we produce a movie for $10 million, and our distributor spends another $7 million on publicity, and the movie makes $75 million at the box office and another $50 million in the video stores, it certainly is worth it.

A great deal of what is delineated here will become a distribution expense, not attributable to our budget. Print ads generally are handled by the distributor and exhibitor, as is almost all post-production publicity. So be aware that these are guidelines, not cast in concrete.

6301   Unit Publicist

Description	Amount	Units	X	Rate	Subtotal
Prep	0	Week	1	1,495.31	0
Shoot	4	Weeks	1	1,495.31	5,981
Wrap	0	Week	1	1,495.31	0
					5,981
Overtime allowance	10	%	1	0	0
Personal Equipment Rental	10	Weeks	1	0	0
Car Allowance	0	Week	1	0	0
Total					**5,981**

Window chrome text: Movie Magic Budgeting [BUDBOOK.MMB — 6301 — Publicist]; File Edit Setup Tools Library Go To Magic Window Help; BUDBOOK.MMB 2,671,976; Category 6300 27,857; Account 6301 5,981; Cume: 0; Change: 0; TOP SHEET ACCOUNT DETAIL.

The Unit Publicist is a witty, personable soul whose purpose is to ensure that the film and its personnel are mentioned in as many publications as often as possible. In his or her zeal, the Publicist usually schedules a whole crew from *Entertainment Tonight* to visit the set and disrupt filming on the one day when nothing is photographically interesting and the Director has requested that the set be closed because of the emotionality of the scene. On the other hand, 90 percent of the publicists I have worked with have been extremely responsible about scheduling the press visits to the set.

Many years ago I was working on the lot at 20th Century-Fox when a fire started in the mill. Sirens screamed, traffic control officers ran to the mill, all that combustible material was lying around, and it was a mess. I happened to be working nearby so I walked over. As I approached, a famous movie star drove up in his limousine, emerged from the back seat, removed his jacket and shirt (baring his chest), took a fire hose from a fireman, and sprayed the fire long enough for the reporters to take his picture. He handed the hose back to the fireman, put back his shirt and jacket, got into his limo and left. You'll never guess whose picture was on the front page of the next morning newspaper.

6304   Still Photographer

Description	Amount	Units	X	Rate	Subtotal	
Prep	0	Week	1	0	0	
Shoot	0	Weeks	1	0	0	
Wrap	0	Week	1	0	0	
					0	
Overtime allowance	10	%	1	0	0	
Personal Equipment Rental	0	Weeks	1	0	0	
Car Allowance	0	Week	1	0	0	
Film/Lab	0		1	0	0	
Total					**0**	

Movie Magic Budgeting - [BUDBOOK.MMB - 6304 - Stillsman]
File Edit Setup Tools Library Go To Magic Window Help

BUDBOOK.MMB   2,671,976
Category 6300   27,857
Account 6304   0

Cume: 0
Change: 0

The Still Photographer in feature films usually is a regular member of the crew. He or she is assigned exclusively to one show and is present for all filming. Remember, the more exposure in the press we get the more audience we can expect, as a general rule. And we never know when a photo opportunity will present itself. So keeping a Still Photographer on the set is cheap insurance.

In TV it works differently. The Network publicity department usually assigns a Photographer to a unit for a specific number of days, usually when filming the most spectacular stunts or special effects or when the guest cameo Star is present, but the Photographer is not there all the time. So, as a Producer, you have to choose the days when you feel the best photographs will be possible, let the Network know, and hope it all works out that way.

6307   Public Relations Fee

We may wish to engage a public relations firm to handle the publicity. In that case, a fee is negotiated and the firm engaged handles all the logistics of the publicity. The firm will hire a publicist or assign one of its own for the show, handle the stills, plant items in the media, and generally take over the whole publicity shebang for us.

6308   Design Work

Description	Amount	Units	X	Rate	Subtotal
Logo Designs	0		1	0	0
Art Work/Layouts	0		1	0	0
Stationery Printing	0		1	0	0
Special Art Work	0		1	0	0
Special Layouts	0		1	0	0
Special Printing	0		1	0	0
Total					**0**

BUDBOOK.MMB 2,671,976 — Category 6300 27,857 — Account 6308 0 — Cume: 0 — Change: 0

At some point we may wish to design a logo for the show or have some art work done.

Logo: The odd design that signifies to everyone our work. The logo for Shell Oil Company is a yellow scallop shell, familiar to anyone who drives U.S. highways.

6400 Miscellaneous

Acct#	Account Title	Page	Total
6401	Accounting Fees	75	0
6402	Bank Service Charges	75	0
6403	Foreign Money Exchange	75	0
6404	Bank Loan Interest	75	0
6405	Taxes & Licenses	75	0
6406	MPAA Code Certification	75	0
6407	Finders Fees	75	0
6408	General Office Expenses	75	0
6409	Executive Entertainment	76	0
6410	Executive Travel/Lodging	76	0
6411	Studio Executive Tvl/Lodg	76	0
6412	Preview Expenses	76	0
6413	Cast/Crew Expenses	76	0
6414	Miscellaneous	76	0
6499	**Total Fringes**		**0**
	Total		**0**

There always has to be a miscellaneous account, doesn't there? Otherwise, where would we put everything we can't put anywhere else?

6401   Accounting Fees

We may wish to hire an accounting firm to handle our picture. We can cut a weekly or monthly deal with an accounting firm or we can work on an all-in fee situation. Sometimes, especially with movies of the week, the last option is the best; long after the show has been edited there will still be residuals to pay for second run, syndication, and so forth. In an all-in deal the accounting firm will still be working for us even though the actual accountants who worked our show will have moved on to other shows.

This account would apply to our own company's accounting firm, not to the Production Accountant (Account 2114) who is handling only this one project.

6402   Banking Fees

Banks are notorious for suddenly coming up with obscure reasons to take our money.

6403   Foreign Exchange

Once again, when we change U.S. money into drachmas or whatever, we inevitably lose something in the translation. Then we will lose even more when we try to change drachmas back into dollars. We also may run into situations in which foreign countries have such fantastically high inflation rates that our money has lost its value while we were filming. This is a situation to try to avoid if possible. Being stuck in a foreign country with worthless money can be very disquieting.

6405 Taxes and Licenses

Description	Amount	Units	X	Rate	Subtotal
Federal Corp. Taxes	0		1	0	0
State Corp. Taxes	0		1	0	0
State Equip't Rental Tax	0		1	0	0
Property Tax	0		1	0	0
Out-of-State Local Taxes	0		1	0	0
Foreign Country Taxes	0		1	0	0
City Business Licenses	0		1	0	0
Out-of State Business Lic	0		1	0	0
Total					**0**

(BUDBOOK.MMB 2,671,976, Category 6400 0, Account 6405 0, Cume: 0, Change: 0)

The state, local, and federal governments will want to relieve us of some cash for doing business in their territories. If we have to go out of state for a period of time and must open a local bank account to pay the local crew and talent, we will probably have to pay for a local business license.

In fact, wherever we film, if we are using the city streets for commerce of any kind we will need a business license for that use. Parking our trucks on the street for filming inside a house is a legitimate use of the street, and the city will want its license fee.

6406 MPAA Code Certification Fee
You will need the MPAA Code Certificate you want to obtain a legitimate release for the movie.

MPAA: Motion Picture Association of America.

6407 Finders Fees
If we have raised the money privately to finance a film, we must pay the person who put us together with the funding parties. This payment, normally a percentage of the money raised, is known as a *Finder's Fee*. The usual rate is 10 percent, but it can vary widely from that mark.

6412 Preview Expenses
We may wish to have a press preview for the film. This is a screening at a sumptuous screening room, such as the Directors Guild Theatre, immediately prior to the public release of the picture. We invite the press so that they can regale the public on this evening's TV news or in tomorrow

morning's paper with the grand time they had watching our film, thereby swelling the audience and our bank account.

6413 Cast and Crew Expenses

Description	Amount	Units	X	Rate	Subtotal
Wrap Party Costs	0		1	0	0
Gifts, Tee-Shirts, Etc.	0		1	0	0
Screenings	0		1	0	0
Total					**0**

Cast and Crew Wrap Party

This can be anything from some chips 'n' dips at the end of the last day of filming to a full party with entertainment and an open bar. It is traditional to do something for the crew, the people who helped us to make the show possible.

Gifts, T-Shirts, and the Like

We might wish to give the crew, staff, and cast members of a film something to remember the film by. The bill for this normally is paid by the Producers personally, and in more than one case I remember by a major Actor. But at times the company will foot the bill for this one. It can be anything from a mug with the movie's logo to a hat or a sweatshirt or jacket.

Contractuals

This ends the main body of the budget. We have a few little details to clear up still. First are the contractuals.

Acct#	Category Title	Page	Total
6400	Miscellaneous	75	0
	TOTAL OTHER		**27,857**
	Completion Bond: 0.00%		**0**
	Contingency: 0.00%		**0**
	Overhead: 0.00%		**0**
	Insurance: 0.00%		**0**
	Total Below-The-Line		**1,779,405**
	Total Above and Below-The-Line		**1,902,866**
	Grand Total		**1,902,866**

These charges are applied as a percentage of the entire direct cost of the film with certain exceptions.

Let's assume that our completion bond will cost 5 percent of the total direct cost of the picture, without the cost of the script and post-production. So first we go to the top sheet.

Acct#	Category Title	Page	Total
1100	Development	1	1,000
1200	Story & Other Rights	2	0
1300	Continuity & Treatment	3	11,619
1400	Producers Unit	4	84,800
1500	Directors Unit	5	26,041
1600	Talent	6	0
1700	A-T-L Travel/Living	6	0
	TOTAL ABOVE-THE-LINE		**123,460**
2100	Production Staff	8	180,641
2200	Art Direction	12	71,200
2300	Set Construction	15	26,969
2400	Set Decoration	18	125,019
2500	Property Department	20	39,460
2600	Camera Operations	22	203,446
2700	Electric Operations	25	128,672
2800	Grip Operations	27	103,266
2900	Production Sound	29	43,328
3000	Mechanical Effects	30	10,379
3100	Special Visual Effects	32	0
3200	Set Operations	33	60,151

Here we note that the script costs are $11,619. Now we scroll down to the post-production line.

Acct#	Category Title	Page	Total
5400	Music	64	0
5500	Titles	65	0
5600	Opticals	65	0
5700	Post-Production Video	68	0
5800	Facilities	71	0
5900	Post-Prod Travel/Living	71	0
	TOTAL POST PRODUCTION		**363,743**

Our post-production total is $363,743. Add to this our script cost of $11,619, and we have a total of $375,362. That is what we exclude from our computation.

Next we scroll down to the bottom of the topsheet:

Acct#	Category Title	Page	Total
6400	Miscellaneous	75	0
	TOTAL OTHER		**27,857**
	Completion Bond: 0.00%		**0**
	Contingency: 0.00%		**0**
	Overhead: 0.00%		**0**
	Insurance: 0.00%		**0**
	Total Below-The-Line		**1,779,405**
	Total Above and Below-The-Line		**1,902,866**
	Grand Total		**1,902,866**

You can see that the arrow is in the left-hand margin of the page, opposite the Completion Bond line. We highlight that line and double-click with the left button:

Acct#	Category Title	Page	Total
6400	Miscellaneous	75	0
	TOTAL OTHER		**27,857**
	Completion Bond: 0.00%		**0**
	Contingency: 0.00%		**0**
	Overhead: 0.00%		**0**
	Insurance: 0.00%		**0**
	Total Below-The-Line		**1,779,405**
	Total Above and Below-The-Line		**1,902,866**
	Grand Total		**1,902,866**

That action brings us to this screen:

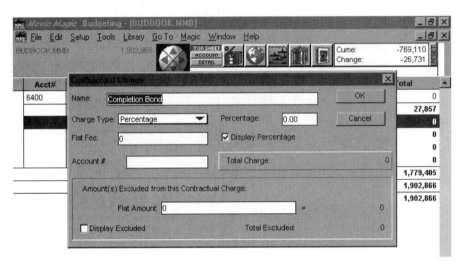

First, we insert our percentage into the "Percentage" window, then we add the exclusion figure we just calculated into the "Amount excluded" window.

Note that the program automatically figured in the 5 percent in the "Flat Fee" window. Then we can click on the "OK" button:

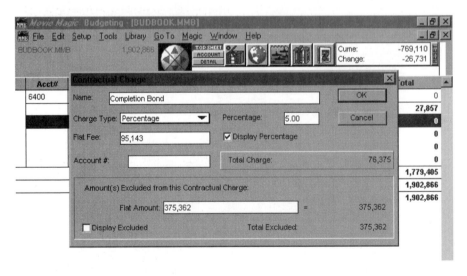

And, voilà, back at the top sheet our percentage has been calculated for us automatically.

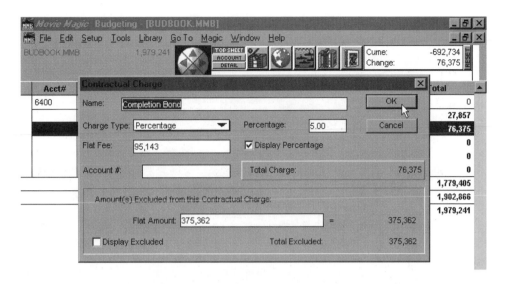

We likewise will calculate all the rest of our contractuals. First we need a figure for Contingency. So we double-click the "Contingency" line:

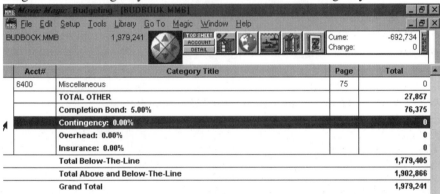

In the "Percentage" window on the resulting screen we put a 10. Note that we do not put in an exclusion figure because we are using the whole cost as a basis for calculating the contingency, not excluding anything.

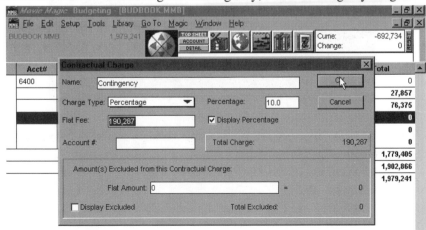

We click on the OK button and have our contingency on the top sheet:

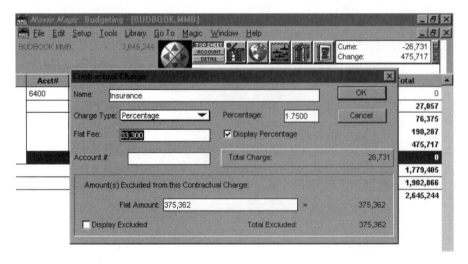

We handle the Overhead in a similar way. Overhead in the case of the major studios can be as much as 25 percent of the total direct costs without exclusions. Someone has to pay for all the Janitors who clean the studio grounds, the soap in the restrooms, and oh yes, the Studio Executives' salaries.

This leaves Insurance. We could either have filled in Account 6100, or we can make an estimate on the top sheet as we do here. Usually I just estimate on the top sheet. I usually calculate insurance at 1.75 percent of the total direct cost excluding the same figure we used in the Completion Bond palette:

So now the bottom of our top sheet looks like this:

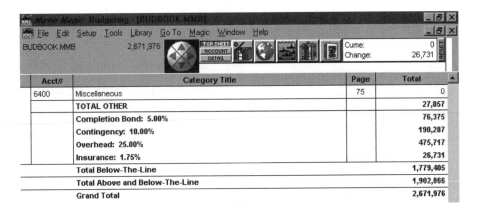

If we wish, by checking the appropriate box, we can even make the exclusions evident:

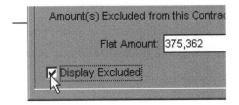

As we can see, we have put a check mark in the Display Excluded box to make the exclusions evident. Now the top sheet has them shown:

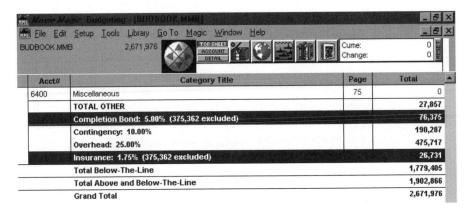

We have highlighted those two lines to make them more evident.

We still have to address another area to explain the budget process:

Fringe Benefits

Name	Description	I.D.	Percent	Cutoff	Total
FICA			6.200	65400	61,817
FUI			0.800	7000	4,189
SUI			5.00	7000	26,182
Workmen's Comp			3.9800	0	40,104
Medicare			1.4500	0	14,611
Payroll Svc.			0.500	0	4,975

Fringe Benefits by Flat Rate per Unit

Name	Description	I.D.	Rate	Units	Cutoff	Total
IATSE	IATSE		2.3625	Hours	0	51,370
Teamsters	Teamsters		2.3625	Hours	0	3,402

There are two kinds of fringe benefits: payroll taxes and union fringe benefits.

Payroll taxes are those we must pay the government on behalf of the employee. These are based on a percentage of the employee's salary, and they almost always have a maximum income, or cutoff, beyond which further benefits need not be paid.

FICA

This is the **F**ederal **I**nsurance **C**ontribution **A**ct or Social Security. The employer contributes the equivalent of 6.2 percent of the employee's salary to the government for social security, up to a maximum income of $65,400. After that the company stops its contributions.

FUI

Federal Unemployment Insurance. The US Government insists that companies pay the equivalent of .8 percent (that's 8/10 of 1 percent) of the employee's income toward federal unemployment insurance, to a maximum income of $7,000.

SUI

California State Unemployment Insurance. The SUI figure, also with a maximum income of $7,000, varies from state to state. We must be careful when we film out of state that the figures are proper.

Workers Compensation

In the unlikely event that an employee is injured on the job, the company has donated the equivalent of 3.98 percent of the employee's income, no maximum, toward the government insurance fund to care for him. Sometimes, this is included in the total insurance package and need not be included here. Also, 3.98 percent is a maximum figure. Projects with few stunts or special effects might be paying a smaller percentage because the risk is less.

Medicare

This is everyone's favorite fringe benefit. As the United States edges slowly toward the status of welfare state, we will find more of this sort of tax. It is 1.45 percent, no cutoff.

Payroll Service

Payroll Service is not a tax. I added it into the budget to make it easier to calculate how much we will be paying our payroll service. Unless we are working at a major studio with its own payroll service or unless we elect to pay our own payroll, we will be hiring one of the many payroll services in town to handle this chore for us. And these folks will be charging a small fee based on a percentage of the payroll flowing through their office. Usually ½ percent or less.

Name	Description	I.D.	Percent	Cutoff	Total
Payroll Svc.			0.500	0	4,975
WGA			12.500	202000	0
DGA			13.00	250000	11,479
Vacation/Holiday			7.71900	0	67,938
SAG			13.300	200000	0
Trust A/C	IATSE. Teamster Trust Account		1	0	0

Setup Fringes for "BUDBOOK.MMB" — Add — Remove — **Fringe Benefits by Percentage** — Cancel — OK

The next batch of fringe benefits are the employer's share of contributions to the various Unions and Guilds. These vary with each entity, but all dance around the 12.5 percent figure, some more, some less. Some have greater cutoffs, some less.

WGA: The Writers Guild of America
DGA: The Directors Guild of America
SAG: Screen Actors Guild
IATSE: International Alliance of Theatrical Stage Employees

The IATSE and Teamsters have a **Trust account** to which employers must contribute 1 percent of the earned income of the employees.

Vacation and Holiday Pay

This is a little bonus for what management assumes will be a few days off between pictures. It is contributed by the employer, at 7.719 percent of the employee's total income. This applies to the DGA, IATSE, and the Teamsters.

Name	Description	I.D.	Percent	Cutoff	Total
Vacation/Holiday			7.71900	0	67,938
SAG			13.300	200000	0
Trust A/C	IATSE. Teamster Trust Account		1	0	0
Overtime	Overtime Allowance		0	0	0
State Sales Tax			8.2500	0	1,449

Setup Fringes for "BUDBOOK MMB" — Add / Remove — Fringe Benefits by Percentage — Cancel / OK

There are two entries in the fringe area which are not, strictly speaking, fringe benefits.

Overtime

I generally estimate overtime on a picture as a percentage of the employee's salary and this usually is accurate. Note that under each crew member in the main body of the budget is an Overtime line, so we can estimate overtime in one place or the other. I find the percentage calculation to be easier.

State Sales Tax

I have used this handy means to apply state sales tax to all items purchased during the shoot. In California the amount is 8.25 percent. In other states it is greater or lesser. We will adjust our budgets accordingly.

Name	Description	I.D.	Rate	Units	Cutoff	Total
IATSE	IATSE		2.3625	Hours	0	51,370
Teamsters	Teamsters		2.3625	Hours	0	3,402

Add / Remove — Fringe Benefits by Flat Rate per Unit

Another kind of fringe benefit calculation is a *flat rate* calculation. In this case, the employee receives a set amount per hour worked no matter what the salary might be. The D.P. and Craft Service Person both get $2.3625 per hour worked, even though one might make $10,000 per week and the other $1500 per week.

Movie Magic Budgeting can accommodate both kinds of fringe benefits properly.

Finis

This brings us to the end of our budget. It's been some journey – rather reminds me of a line Mr. Hardy used to say to Mr. Laurel: "A lot of weather we've been having lately, isn't it?"

Questions or comments may be addressed to the publisher, who will pass them along to me. Or you can e-mail me at: rkoster@leonardo.net.

Be sure to visit my web site at: http://www.leonardo.net/starcomp.

Happy budgeting!

Index

ABOUT THE ACCOMPANYING CD-ROM

This is a FULLY FUNCTIONAL, DUAL-PLATFORM CD-ROM containing an annotated version of MOVIE MAGIC BUDGETING SOFTWARE. For demonstration purposes, the saving, printing, and library features have been disabled.

SYSTEM REQUIREMENTS:

PC
- Windows 3.1 or Higher
- 386 or Better CPU with 6 MB of Available RAM
- 10 MB of Available Hard Disk Space
- CD-ROM Drive

MACINTOSH
- System 7.0 or Better
- 6 MB of Available RAM (May Use Virtual Memory)
- 10 MB of Available Hard Disk Space
- CD-ROM Drive